Praise
The Four O'Clc

"A useful and urgent manual for teachers who care. People like you."

—SETH GODIN, AUTHOR OF *STOP STEALING DREAMS*

"Rich's book is for any educator who has suffered through Professional Development (PD) meetings, sessions, or days that had no planning or no effort to make the time or process relevant to the participants. Rich's direct approach to making PD valuable is refreshing. The advice on the use of Twitter and building Professional Learning Networks is exceptional. All of us who have resorted to playing 'PD Bingo' during in-service will find this gem extremely worthwhile. Use it yourself but share it with colleagues and administrators. This book is a classic for all educational leaders who wish to provide appropriate and participatory PD."

—MICHAEL CURRAN, EDUCATORS VOICE
COLLEGE PROFESSOR OF THE YEAR

"*The Four O'Clock Faculty* has been a morning eye-opener for me for over a year. In his book, Rich Czyz has shared some amazing ideas to give life to professional development and professional learning for educators. His ideas are practical and unique. Teachers can take charge of their own learning starting today. Administrators can use this book to re-charge their meetings and PD days. This is Rich's manifesto. Never let a day go by without learning. Thank you for writing and sharing your amazing ideas."

—JAY BILLY, PRINCIPAL

"Rich Czyz's masterful new book is an insider's view of professional learning at its finest with a flexible step-by-step roadmap of try-it-tomorrow options. Rich keeps his promise of personalized, relevant and connected PD by sharing his vision to redefine, reimagine and redesign PD. *The Four O'Clock Faculty* will transform the face of PD by creating a culture of meaningful, productive and respectful conversations that will allow countless educators to bring his promise to life where it matters most – in the company of children."

—DR. MARY HOWARD, EDUCATIONAL CONSULTANT
AND AUTHOR OF *GOOD TO GREAT TEACHING*

"Rich Czyz does a tremendous job of providing professional learning ideas and strategies that can be implemented with ease and enhance educator effectiveness. *The Four O'Clock Faculty* is great for any educator looking to promote the success of students at the classroom, school, and district level."

—BRAD CURRIE, 2017 NASSP NATIONAL
ASSISTANT PRINCIPAL OF THE YEAR

"Professional development doesn't have to be boring! If you lead or plan professional development, Rich provides practical, engaging ideas to kick professional learning up to the next level. This is a handbook of relevant PD ideas you'll want to refer to over and over."

—MATT MILLER, AUTHOR OF *DITCH THAT TEXTBOOK*

"If we are going to shape education to prepare students for the future of work, school leaders have to start at the top by changing the paradigm of professional growth for teachers. Rich offers meaningful and pragmatic solutions to do just this, including wonderful anecdotes that share the success he has experienced in his work."

—RICH KIKER, PARTNER, GOOGLE FOR EDUCATION

"It is imperative that twenty-first-century educators take ownership of their professional learning. In this book, Mr. Czyz helps to redefine what it means for educators to learn professionally and highlights a variety of practical resources each teacher can adopt to expand his or her professional practice."

—LAURA FLEMING, AUTHOR OF *THE KICKSTART GUIDE TO MAKING GREAT MAKERSPACES*

"The Four O' Clock Faculty is a book that I wish I had when beginning my journey as a principal. It is filled with practical strategies that can be implemented with any group of adult learners. Rich takes ideas that we know are best practice in classrooms and adjusts to meet the needs of adults. I highly recommend this go-to resource for all that are looking to transform their PD practices."

—BETH HOUF, PRINCIPAL, FULTON MIDDLE SCHOOL CO-AUTHOR OF *LEAD LIKE A PIRATE: MAKE SCHOOLS AMAZING FOR YOUR STUDENTS AND STAFF*

"Only read this book if you want people to be awake, excited and alert at your next PD event. But I'm warning you, once you read this book your staff is going to be asking for more PD days. Are you ready for that?"

—JON HARPER, HOST OF *MY BAD* PODCAST

"*The Four O'Clock Faculty* arms administrators and professional development teams with exactly the tools and the mindset they need for change in their schools. Teaching has changed. School has changed. Rich understands these changes deeply and provides examples from quick turnaround ideas to long-term PD that can have a lasting impact. Rich has a great sense of humor and clearly knows how to develop great relationships with his staff. You'll develop a relationship with this book that can take your school's professional development to new, real places of growth."

—DENIS SHEERAN, AUTHOR OF *INSTANT RELEVANCE*

The Four O'Clock Faculty

A ~~Practical~~ Rogue
Guide to
Revolutionizing
Professional
Development

Rich Czyz

The Four O'Clock Faculty
© 2017 by Richard Czyz

> This book is available at special discounts when purchased in quantity for use as premiums, promotions, fundraisers, or for educational use. For inquiries and details, contact the publisher at books@daveburgessconsulting.com.

Published by Dave Burgess Consulting, Inc.
San Diego, CA
http://daveburgessconsulting.com

Cover Design by Genesis Kohler
Editing and Interior Design by My Writers' Connection

Library of Congress Control Number:
Paperback ISBN: 978-1-946444-36-3
Ebook ISBN: 978-1-946444-37-0

First Printing: July 2017

Dedication

To my wife for her never-ending support and love.

To my children who inspire me each and every day.

To my parents who raised me with a sense
of professional responsibility and duty.

Thank you.

Contents

Introduction

We are a four o'clock faculty.

—ROY BRIGGS

I am on a mission, and I want you to join me. My aim is to change the face of professional learning for educators. It is well past time to make this happen. If you agree to join me on this adventure, I can promise you a few things:

- You will become a better educator.

- You will learn new ways to engage not only yourself but also your colleagues and students.

- You will become the most popular educator among your peers.

(Okay, let's be honest. This last one might or might not happen. It's actually possible you could upset some people, but it is important to note that everything you do to improve your own learning helps you become the best educator *you* can be. So go ahead and give yourself permission to ignore the naysayers.)

Now that we have that out of the way and you're still reading, I hope you share the conviction that motivated me to write this book: Pursuing learning and professional development is the single most important action we can take to hone our craft as educators.

We hear the term *lifelong learner* mentioned in education circles all the time. We want to be lifelong learners, and we want our students to grow up to become lifelong learners. But how many of us are living that out? How are you and the educators you know intentionally and consistently pursuing learning?

The truth is, professional development (PD) often falls to one or two district or building administrators. But if we are to improve as educators, it is imperative that each of us takes responsibility for our own professional learning. As educators, we must continually be on the lookout for opportunities on and off campus to stretch ourselves professionally.

As we begin this journey, let me tell you how I got started on my own path to improve professional learning for myself and my colleagues. I currently serve as a principal of a small second- and third-grade building in New Jersey. In my fifteen years of education, I have been a classroom teacher, basic skills interventionist, technology and instructional coach, and a Supervisor and Director of Curriculum and Instruction. In my roles, I have been responsible for planning and presenting professional development sessions and have seen the good, the bad, and the ugly. Throughout it all, I continue to be as passionate today about professional learning as I was when I first started, and I have continued to engage in my own professional learning.

If you're a teacher, it's likely you have experienced a few less-than-stellar professional development sessions that had little to no relevance to what you do every day. Some might argue that every opportunity to expand your knowledge base has some merit, even if you might not be in a position to apply that knowledge on a daily basis. But educators, I believe, are like most practitioners: We want to perfect our individual and specific skills. To that end, it's critical that we obtain knowledge and information that directly supports the work we do day to day; for example, why do we force music and art teachers to sit through mandatory training in math instruction? This happens more often than I would like to admit, so we need to ask this question: Why should teachers settle for training that's irrelevant to their roles in the classroom?

I experienced this frustration early in my teaching career. My district was implementing a new writing assessment, and it had established a year-long training program for teachers using the new assessment. In one sense, I must applaud the district for rolling out a new initiative with a comprehensive training program. Some school districts would have provided teachers one workshop on the new writing rubric, and that would have been the end of it. The fact that teachers were sitting together once a month to learn about the program was commendable—sort of. At the time, I taught fifth-grade math and science, so the new writing rubric had no relevance to my daily role. The rubric was going to be used only in language arts classes. So there I sat in the training, a math teacher learning about a writing rubric I was never going to use. I sat between two colleagues, one who also taught fifth-grade math and science and one who taught kindergarten through fifth-grade art. Within our group, the number of times we would use the new writing rubric to score a student's written work would be zero. This fact was not lost on any of us, especially me.

After each meeting, I walked slowly back to my classroom with my colleagues, complaining about the training the entire way. "Why do I need to sit and listen to professional development about a rubric that I am never going to use?" I wondered aloud. "Can't they realize this is a huge waste of time for some of us?" My resentment took over, and I didn't even try to learn anything from those sessions or apply any of the insights to my teaching methods. Looking back, I can now admit that was a critical mistake on my part, but that frustration ultimately helped me become the educator I am today. At the time, however, although I recognized the problem, I did nothing to work toward a solution. I didn't try to find a more relevant use of my time. In fact, I let my valuable time be wasted by assuming my professional development was someone else's responsibility.

After almost a year of making excuses, I finally decided to challenge the status quo. I explained to my principal that the training had nothing to do with allowing me to help my kids and asked to meet with colleagues to discuss our math curriculum. Up to this point, we felt we had been racing through the math pacing guide, hitting topic after topic, but never giving students a true conceptual understanding of the foundations of math or how it applied to them. We wanted to give students more context for how the math skills they were learning could be applied in real-life examples. Deep down, I believe that my principal recognized that we were not helping our students in math with such a school-wide focus on writing. After nine months of sitting through the writing sessions, we were granted the last meeting in June to meet to discuss the math curriculum. We gathered to discuss and start creating real-life word problem examples, something that would take the students from math theory and isolated skills to real-world application. The session in June led to additional sessions the following year, and a renewed focus on quality math instruction. It was a small win, but a win nonetheless. And more importantly, it served as a bigger win for our students. The following year, we were able to provide real-world problems where students could take the skills they were learning and apply them. Taking that stand was one of the key moments that led to my determination to improve professional development, not only for myself but others as well. At the time, I didn't know my long-term goals included administration, but I knew that if I were ever in charge, I would never make anyone sit through a session that had no relevance to them or their daily work.

A few years later, I took a leadership position in a new district. My midyear arrival was just in time to attend an in-service day on the Friday of President's Day weekend. Now, I have never researched the term *in-service* and don't know the history of the phrase, but it doesn't sound at all interesting, relevant, or meaningful. Evidently, I'm not the only one with that impression.

On the day of in-service training, the teachers shuffled into mandated sessions featuring large-group presentations. It was the traditional sit-and-get model with little interaction between the audience and the instructor. All teachers were required to take part in a mandatory dyslexia training session. Everyone was forced to learn about new math and language arts standards, even those who taught other subject areas. Teachers were frustrated. I heard several teachers echo as they walked out of the final session, "What a waste of time!!!" Although I had only been in the district a few short months, it was easy to see teachers were not getting what they needed.

I also discovered another interesting fact that day. After searching the campus for one particular teacher—and striking out with several people—someone informed me, "Oh, she took off today."

"Took off?"

"Yeah, a lot of teachers take off in-service days to make it a four-day weekend."

Taking off on a professional day? It was the first time I had ever heard of such a thing. Was that even allowed? In my previous districts, it hadn't been an option. I was shocked that some teachers would consider skipping professional development, but after some serious reflection, I realized I couldn't blame them. If leaders don't provide relevant professional development, then why should teachers show up? Why wouldn't they decide their time was better spent somewhere else?

More than ever, I became convinced that the culture of professional learning needed to change, not only in my own school district but for educators everywhere. We needed to change the system from the inside out.

Extremely difficult? Yes.

A lot of work? No doubt.

A challenge? In every way.

Impossible? No.

I racked my brain trying to think where and how to begin this shift toward more individualized and meaningful professional development. What could I do to change professional learning? How could I, as one educator, possibly make an impact? I quickly realized I would need some help, and so I reached out to my good friend and fellow educator Trevor Bryan. We had been colleagues at a brand-new school many years ago. I was the rookie, fresh out of a teacher certification program, and Trevor was hired as the art teacher. We shared a passion for education and learning as much as we could to improve what was happening in our classrooms. Through the years, Trevor shared with me many stories about his father, Larry Bryan, who also was an educator. Larry had done it all in education, serving students for thirty-eight years as a teacher, supervisor, and assistant superintendent. One story has always stayed with me, and it speaks to that responsibility administrators have in helping their teachers become the best they can be.

In 1959, Joel Barlow High School opened in Redding, Connecticut. Roy Briggs was the first principal. Briggs recognized his situation as a unique opportunity; not many principals have the chance to hand-pick each member of their faculty. Briggs' aim was not only to hire the best teachers he could find but to hire a faculty that would help establish the high school as the best in the state. He hired Larry Bryan as a teacher in 1960. During his interview, Briggs informed Bryan the school day ended at 2:15 p.m. When Bryan asked, "What time can teachers leave?" Briggs simply responded, "We are a four o'clock faculty."

An hour and forty-five minutes might not seem like much time to devote to improvement, but the idea resonated with me, and I decided to follow Roy Briggs' lead.

And so, Four O'Clock Faculty was born.

The mission was simple: We wanted to establish something that would allow all educators to be the best that they could be. We wanted to engage educators who wanted to improve schools and learning—for themselves and their students—in meaningful, relevant work. Educators must pride themselves on doing whatever is necessary to improve learning.

The mission of the Four O'Clock Faculty extends beyond the walls of any school. In fact, if you are unhappy with the professional learning opportunities made available to you, now is the time for you to join the Four O'Clock Faculty. It's simple:

1. Commit to becoming the best educator that you can be. Forget all the naysayers.
2. Commit yourself to learning as much as you can so your students can learn as much as they can.
3. Start now by reading the rest of this book.

The Road Ahead

Before you move forward, here's a quick look at where we're headed:

In Section 1, we will look at what professional development is, what it could be, and why all educators have a responsibility to ensure that we are continually growing as professionals. We will examine how some professional development ends up as one-size-fits-all, and you will learn several principles for better PD, such as how a simple CHOICE between two learning sessions can impact an educator's attitude toward professional learning.

Section 2 offers practical strategies that you can use almost immediately to impact learning outcomes for your students. We will examine ways to maximize available time for professional learning; for example, what do you currently do with the fifteen minutes before students arrive? How about the fifteen minutes after students leave? Learn how to take advantage of this time! We will also explore ways to take advantage of technology to connect with expanded professional learning opportunities or to explore PD opportunities on your own.

Section 3 will help us as we all move forward with professional learning by exploring how we can redefine professional learning communities and by providing a game plan for changing professional development. We will answer the question, "What do I do when my professional learning experience is terrible?" and you can learn how to PDIY (PD It Yourself). We will also show you how you can go beyond learning in order to solve a problem or create something meaningful.

Within this book, you will find several strategies, structures, and resources for redesigning professional learning. The ideas apply to anyone who wants to use them. You might be an administrator looking to refuel your teachers through new dynamic professional development opportunities. You might be a teacher seeking ways to connect with like-minded individuals who share your passion for learning. You might be an instructional coach who is not getting what you need in terms of professional development. Or you might be like me, an educator who is dedicated to learning and growing so students get the teacher they need—and deserve.

Now is the time to redesign professional learning for all educators. Our students need us to be at our best. And for our own sanity and success, *we* need to pursue relevant, meaningful learning that empowers us to thrive as educators.

Thank you for joining me on this journey.

Section 1

What PD Was Meant to Be

Chapter One
Choosing to Pursue Relevant PD

You don't learn to walk by following rules.
You learn by doing, and by falling over.

—RICHARD BRANSON

I would like to believe that most professional development is devised and presented with good intentions. It's not as if school leaders sit down to plan teacher learning sessions and say, "Let's make this as boring and painful as possible. We'll gather everyone in one room and talk *at* them for at least an hour about something that doesn't relate to their jobs. Let's make sure they leave feeling unfulfilled and uninspired, and that their spirit is completely broken!"

As a former teacher who moved into administration, I believe that I have a good understanding of how professional development should work. I have sat through good and bad professional development sessions as a participant, and I have been responsible for planning both good and bad professional development days as an administrator.

It pains me to say it, but I understand why some professional development is in such a dismal state. The truth is that those who are tasked with planning professional development for most school districts are placed in an incredibly difficult position. In addition to fulfilling training requirements mandated by state and local agencies, these leaders deal with time limitations, dwindling funding, and contractual issues. Sometimes finding adequate space or suitable venues is a problem.

Add to those challenges the knowledge that their staff members are likely to resist *any* kind of PD sessions because they have a thousand other things on their minds and are being asked to give up their valuable time for a day of (potentially boring or irrelevant) training, and you can see how planning the "perfect" PD might seem impossible. I can tell you from experience that the reason many administrators plan one-size-fits-all professional development is that it is easier and safer than planning meaningful and relevant learning opportunities for targeted audiences.

Let me run through a scenario: Say your school or district has a professional development session coming up in one month, and you are responsible for planning it. The educators in your school or district will finish early and have ninety minutes of PD time after students leave for the day. You have two options for planning:

Option A

Present state-mandated Dyslexia training in the cafetorium. One speaker will share information via seventy-five PowerPoint slides. Your responsibilities are as follows:

- Booking the cafetorium for the afternoon

- Calling to set up the speaker

- Emailing everyone to let them know when and where the training will happen

Option B

Provide a menu of learning choices that includes training for a new technology initiative for educators at various levels of expertise, training for a new math program for teachers who want to differentiate instruction across a spectrum of learners, and training for new science standards and building lessons to measure the required benchmarks. Your responsibilities are as follows:

- Reserve a computer lab or computer cart for the technology training. Ensure Internet access for the teachers who will participate.

- Schedule three different sessions for the new technology initiative—beginner, intermediate, and advanced—and find trainers who can accommodate the skills and comfort levels in each session.

- Contact the company providing the new math program and request a trainer for your session. Although the program is being rolled out across the school district, make sure the trainer covers the elements of the program most relevant to your school's students.

- Find a room to accommodate the math session and have the technology department provide PowerPoint capability.

- Find a room where the school's science teachers can meet to discuss the new curriculum. Lead this session yourself or find a department head or a lead teacher with the ability to decipher and explain the new standards.

- Finalize times and locations for each training session and email the information to every teacher participating.

Now, as the planner, which would you choose? While most of us recognize that Option B is far more likely to be meaningful and relevant to the attendees, many planners have chosen and will continue to choose Option A because it is the safe and easy choice. With fewer options, less can go wrong. But at the same time, there is a whole lot less that can go right.

When leaders base professional development on the needs of the district, the individual schools, *and* on their teachers' needs, they maximize everyone's time and move closer to improved learning outcomes in the classroom. The trouble is that accommodating everyone's needs can be extremely difficult. On the upside, the benefits— empowered and engaged educators and students—are well worth the effort.

My Core Beliefs

During my time as a planner of professional development, I have formed several beliefs about what professional learning should include to be successful. I'm outlining my beliefs here so that the rest of the book makes sense.

- **Professional learning should be meaningful.** Any time educators take the time to sharpen their skills, what they are learning should be relevant and useful to their roles in education; for example, if I am the school nurse and I am required to attend an after-school professional development session, I would like to learn about something that is specific to the daily duties of a school nurse. An excellent session might include preventative measures during flu season or the latest information regarding head trauma and concussions. The best PD is aligned not only to the needs of an individual school but also to those of specific educators and helps both meet their goals.

- **Educators should have a say in what they learn and how they learn it.** Getting my seven-year-old daughter to do homework can feel like pulling teeth; however, if my daughter is reading a book about the solar system, she will gladly sit for hours to learn because it's a topic about which she is passionate. The same is true for adult learners. If teachers have a choice and the freedom to explore subject areas they enjoy, they will be more likely to engage in professional learning. Professional development doesn't have to be choice driven 100 percent of the time. In fact, sometimes choice is not an option, and educators must adhere to national, state, or local professional requirements. But when educators are able to choose courses and workshops best suited to their personal learning styles, they will emerge better equipped to help their own students.

- **Time is a precious thing. As educators, we never have enough of it.** We try to cram everything into a six-and-a-half-hour school day. We work through our lunches. We take home enough work to keep ourselves busy on most nights and weekends.

  At the end of a long day, the last thing most of us want to do is sit through a faculty meeting, even if it's necessary. One of the keys to teacher engagement is to make sure professional development sessions honor the time of the professionals participating. Meetings should start and end on time, and the session time be used for meaningful activities.

- **Lists of policies, reminders, and other forms of one-way communication are best left for emails.** It seems like there's always one administrator whose idea of a great faculty meeting is reading to teachers from a long list of bulleted items. We've all been there. Death by PowerPoint with forty-seven slides that look like this:

Math Collaboration Strategies for Learners

↑ Math Roundtable:

◆ Have students split into groups of 4. Give each group several pieces of blank paper and a stack of sticky notes. Have each student fold the paper into 4 boxes. Each student should write the same problem in each of the 4 boxes. Next, students can rotate through each of the problems, writing their solution in one of the boxes. After solving, students can cover their solution using a sticky note before passing on to another group member. Give students 3 minutes to solve the problem before rotating the papers to solve another problem. After four rotations, the group can remove the sticky notes and compare the solutions to the problems. Critical discussion can focus on any mistakes or differences between solutions.

↑ Fish Bowl:

◆ Set up desks in this model using an inner circle and an outer circle. Students in the inner circle can focus on solving a problem through a think aloud while students in the outside circle focus on the strategies that students in the inner circle are using. Infuse technology in this activity by having the students in the outer circle record their notes using Today's Meet or a shared Google Doc. After the problem solving activity is over, have all students debrief about the strategies used to come to a solution. To stretch student thinking even more, have students switch circles and try to come up with a different solution to the problem.

↑ Collaboration with Other Classrooms:

◆ Technology has made it easy to reach out to experts as well as other teachers and students in classrooms around the world. Utilize technology such as shared Google Docs, Video Conferencing and Blogs to connect with other classrooms. Set up a shared problem solving blog with other classes, allowing your students to connect with students from different cultures and backgrounds. Use Skype or a Google Hangout for discussions and solutions about real-world problems. Have students create and share their own assessments using Google Drive.

The presenter painstakingly reads aloud …
   from …
      each …
         slide …
            word …
               for …
                  word.

By the end, your mind is so numb you can barely figure out how to get home, let alone come up with a great idea or strategy for your students. My general rule of thumb is, if it can be read to your faculty, it belongs in an email.

- **Professional development should focus on improving learning outcomes.** I once planned a PD session for staff members who needed some help getting beyond simple fact-based questions. As an administrator, I typically participate in PD sessions, so I joined in when the presenter said, "Take out a piece of paper and a pen. Is everyone ready? You have one minute. List as many higher-order-thinking questions as you can in one minute. Ready? Go." Several teachers were able to list three questions. Many struggled to come up with one good question. I barely finished one question! The presenter's point was to get the participants to understand the importance of scripting higher-order-thinking questions before a lesson. And it worked. What I loved about the activity is the fact that it changed behaviors with some teachers who began to immediately jot down questions they wanted to ask their students. Aside from this lesson, the session also featured other resources and strategies that staff members could use in their classrooms right away. Getting educators to reflect upon and change their practice so that students benefit should be the goal of *every* PD session.

- **When no one else cares, you should.** Your professional learning is the responsibility of only one person: *you*. While professional development opportunities within your school district may be limited, you have the freedom to attend sessions in other areas. It falls on each one of us to make the most of learning opportunities. If your district is not providing professional development that moves you forward in your field, take charge of your personal learning. Warren Buffett reads five hundred pages per day and often does more with his day before the rest of us have woken up in the morning. I'm not saying you have to read five hundred pages per day. What I am saying is that we should all be as intentional about our ongoing education as we are about our students' learning opportunities. Join the ranks of educators who are serious about improving their skills by reading, collaborating, sharing, discussing, creating, and progressing in your craft every day.

Angry Administrator Update

Not every administrator believes in personalized or self-directed PD. Some think educators should be forced to sit and listen no matter what. These same administrators think it is acceptable to talk *at* their staff members for hours on end, presenting mind-numbing content that makes everyone hate so-called PD. In the rest of this book, I plan to show you that professional development doesn't have to be that way.

Summary

- Professional learning should be meaningful and relevant to an educator's role.

- Educators should have some CHOICE in what and how they learn.

- Professional Development time is precious. It should never be wasted on meaningless activities.

- One-way communication, like lists of policies, bulleted items, and reminders should be emailed to staff members, NOT read to them.

- Professional Development must focus on improved learning outcomes for students.

- YOU have the power to improve your own professional learning!

Reflection Questions

What is your learning style? What types of PD sessions work best for you?

_____

_____

_____

_____

What types of PD have you experienced? Does your school or district tend to implement one type of PD or vary the format and structure?

_____

_____

_____

_____

What are your Core Beliefs about Professional Development?

_____

_____

_____

_____

Section 2

Making PD Relevant

Chapter Two
Learning from Each Other

If you have an apple, and I have an apple, and we exchange apples, then you and I will still each have one apple. But if you have an idea, and I have an idea, and we exchange these ideas, then each of us will have two ideas.

—George Bernard Shaw

A few years ago, I attended my first Edcamp, and it changed my outlook on professional development. I had the opportunity to sit in the same room with several education experts from across the nation and the world who shared their experiences. They talked about strategies that worked and ideas that failed. The conversations that took place that day were exactly that—*conversations*.

Informal and impromptu sessions spawned throughout the day during this "unconference." I attended a session in the morning on changing learning spaces and another session in the afternoon on how to better engage parents in education. I was blown away to learn that teachers from across the country were decorating their classes with couches, bean bags, wobble stools, and other comfortable seating options and giving students choices about where they could sit. It made complete sense to me that students would be better engaged if they were comfortable in the classroom. It also made sense to me that Back to School Night and Parent Conferences were not the only opportunities that we should take advantage of to engage parents. Monthly Coffee with the principal or superintendent can generate valuable discussion from important stakeholders, and a school Twitter or Instagram feed can help to promote the positive things happening in our schools. I was hooked! It was that day that I realized the power of professional learning comes from the ability to have important conversations, reflect on our own questions and concerns, and to share ideas. It became clear to me that once an idea is shared, there is no telling where it might take a person.

After the great experience I had at Edcamp, I realized that the format incorporated all of the conditions for educators to grow professionally. I felt empowered. I had learned a great deal and was ready to bring that learning back to my own district.

"This is what we need to do!" I said to the teacher colleague who had accompanied me. I felt certain we could use elements of the Edcamp model to improve the state of professional development for our local educators.

After four months of planning and many meetings, our District Edcamp was born. It was a modest beginning with two afternoon workshops, each one lasting roughly twenty-five minutes. Teachers could choose between two different topics presented by their colleagues. Many questions arose, and there was some skepticism. Those presenting had to be convinced and weren't sure how they would be received by their colleagues. Some of those in attendance didn't quite understand that they didn't have to attend all four sessions. Some asked how they would receive the information shared in the other sessions if they were not attending (FOMO!). During session A, teachers were able to choose between Strategies to Improve Student Writing or Google Resources. Session B provided options between Executive Functioning or Going Beyond the Worksheet. We wanted the afternoon Edcamp to serve as our proof of concept, and it went well. Teachers were very excited to be able to choose their own sessions and excited to take the strategies they had learned back to the classroom. The biggest complaint was that twenty-five minutes was not nearly enough time.

After proving that this concept could work in our district, my colleagues and I planned a day-long Edcamp-style event built around the concept of sharing. My staff and I worked hard to plan the event. We knew that even though there might be some logistical issues, we needed everyone to have a great experience so the model could live on in the district. Few teachers in our district had experienced a true Edcamp, and we wanted them to understand and benefit from the power of sharing.

A traditional Edcamp event occurs on the weekend. On average, two hundred people attend the events (some driving for several hours to get there)—voluntarily. Rather than sitting in on pre-planned sessions, attendees set up impromptu conversations on a wide variety of topics throughout the weekend.

While our District Edcamp was planned with more structure than traditional Edcamp events, teachers still had the opportunity to choose the session topics that were relevant and meaningful to their daily roles. We knew that requiring three hundred staff members to participate in an Edcamp on a professional development day was very different than educators voluntarily showing up on a Saturday to learn, so we intentionally removed any barriers of uncertainty about the event. We released the schedule before the day of the event to make sure our teachers knew what to expect. On the day of the event, staff members led the different sessions, sharing their expertise with colleagues on topics tied to district goals and encouraging conversation and connection.

All in all, it was a huge success. More than three hundred teachers and instructional aides participated. One teacher called it the "best PD I've ever had." Another teacher said that she would be able to take ideas back with her, as opposed to previous professional development sessions which she felt weren't relevant to her classroom.

If you have attended an Edcamp before, you know all about the power of sharing and connection. If you have not attended and want to consider bringing the idea to your district, here are several critical points to consider when planning an Edcamp-style professional development event in your own district:

- **Remember that Edcamp is a new concept to many educators.** We needed to ensure that everyone understood the format and the goals for the day. Before the event, we worked hard to convey the Edcamp philosophy of sharing and connecting. We showed videos of various Edcamp sessions—Smackdown sessions, which occur at the end of any Edcamp—where educators stand up and share something they learned during the day. We also explained the Rule of Two Feet (which lets educators know that it's okay to walk out of a session if it's not right for you) prior to the day of the workshops to help get teacher buy-in. We wanted them to know exactly what they were getting into before the first workshop started. Remember that our staff members normally attended mandated, whole-group training sessions, so having a choice of discussion topic and being encouraged to openly express ideas and challenges were a big departure from what they were used to.

- **Plan something relevant to all subject areas.** When planning the event, we made a critical decision regarding the structure of the day. In most cases, Edcamp sessions are determined on the day of the event based on the attendees, their needs, and their expertise. We did not want to put staff members on the spot for their first Edcamp experience, so we chose to solicit presenters prior to the event. We created a schedule so educators knew exactly what sessions would be offered and when. I'm proud to say that we had twenty-eight different sessions for our first District Edcamp. Each was offered twice during the day, giving attendees multiple opportunities to join a session. In addition, topics covered a range of subjects, content areas, and interests. In our second year, we were able to offer more than forty different topics taking place during seventy-five different sessions. And while many sessions were pre-scheduled, during the second year's event we allowed time and space for teachers to add additional sessions on the day of the event.

- **Schedule time for sharing throughout the day.** One of my biggest takeaways from the first Edcamp I attended was the number of meaningful conversations that happened between sessions and during lunch. There is no downtime during an Edcamp! With this in mind, we built in plenty of time for collaboration. Each session ran about forty-five minutes, with twenty minutes between sessions for sharing. The Smackdown provided even more time for teachers to interact. In year two, we invited educators from other districts to take part, significantly broadening the scope of conversations.

- **Enlist the help of local and national vendors and businesses.** We were fortunate to have breakfast and coffee donated for our event as well as a number of raffle prizes for attendees. With a little bit of time and effort, we secured classroom technology, gift cards, and other donations. In addition, our Parent Teacher Organization was able to help by providing donations and food for the event.

- **Maximize the day's learning.** Regardless of whether sessions are pre-scheduled, post the links to session resources and notes for each topic after the event. Encourage staff members to come to the event prepared to share a lesson idea, resource, website, strategy, app, or tech tool during the Smackdown session.

In many cases, our participants chose to learn about resources such as apps and websites that they could use in the classroom the next day. In addition, discussion-based sessions led by our guidance counselors and special-education teachers provided participants with ready-to-use behavior strategies. As a result, all of our educators were able to return to their classrooms with practical, useful tools. Each of our presenters was available after the event to continue to talk with educators, so teachers were able to reach out and contact their colleagues if they had additional questions or wanted to follow up on their initial discussions.

My hope is that more educators will host Edcamp events within their own schools or districts. Yes, it requires considerable planning and consideration to the needs of staff, but a District Edcamp can deliver relevant learning and an enjoyable day!

I've since taken a position in a different school district, but the District Edcamp carries on because of the collaborative sharing that takes place. Teachers look forward to the annual event where they have the opportunity to personalize their professional learning experience while focusing on relevant topics and content. The day gives the district an opportunity to implement professional learning that puts teachers at the heart of learning!

When reflecting upon how professional development improved in my previous district, I recognize that the Edcamp model provided important and meaningful learning for teachers. I also learned a few other things:

- **Choice really does matter.** I talked to a number of teachers who were very excited about having the ability to choose which sessions they would attend. Just as choice helps students to become more engaged in the learning process, choice for teachers can support engagement in professional learning. Looking back at the number of PD sessions I have attended over the years, I've come to recognize that the presenter certainly received more buy-in from me when I was engaged in the topic. When I was forced to sit through a session that didn't meet my needs, I was often disinterested at best. At Edcamp, teachers are provided with an opportunity to attend (and even create) a session of their choosing. This choice makes all the difference. Providing a wide variety of workshops and the freedom to choose sessions helps to ensure teachers receive information and resources that are relevant to their classrooms, needs, or interests.

- **Give educators time to share.** We purposefully built in twenty minutes between sessions and a longer lunch period so teachers could share. It was important to us that teachers were truly collaborating and exchanging ideas during the event. Too often teachers are confined to their classrooms, rarely having the opportunity to share with colleagues. Lunchtime often becomes an important meeting time for colleagues. Throughout our District Edcamp, I heard important conversations and reflection going on in the hallways and during lunch. Teachers talked about what they had just learned, shared a lesson idea, and discussed how they would be implementing into their classrooms.

Speaking of which...

- **Teachers are looking for ideas that can be implemented in the classroom immediately.** Much of the sharing at our Smackdown sessions focused on websites, resources, and strategies that teachers were excited to implement in their classrooms. Traditional PD often requires numerous sessions before a teacher can begin implementation in the classroom, but if the point of professional development is to impact students' learning experiences, the content must be relevant and applicable.

- **Educators value learning from their colleagues.** In "one and done" presentations, a presenter from outside the district shares and is not able to provide follow-up. The Edcamp model allows teachers to present their ideas in a collaborative forum and to become an ongoing contact and resource. The exchange of ideas among colleagues helps to inspire development and learning beyond PD sessions. Just as traditional Edcamp events inspire educators to become "connected" using social media, it is important to encourage colleagues to become "connected" with one another as well.

- **Engage your participants with movement and physical interaction.** During traditional professional development, educators are often subjected to two- to three-hour sessions in the same room, with ten-minute stand-and-stretch breaks. It is uncomfortable and hardly conducive to learning something new. During our District Edcamp, teachers moved to a new workshop every forty-five minutes. One session I attended was called "You Too Can Move" and focused on the benefits of including short "brain breaks" in the classroom. Teachers simply provide students with opportunities to stand up between lessons to rejuvenate and engage students throughout the day.

Similarly, sessions on how to create purposeful movement and activity through yoga and through the use of music and story-books helped to illustrate how movement can focus students' attention on content-area skills.

Angry Administrator Update

Be careful in choosing which Edcamps to attend. Some educational leaders have taken the Edcamp name but don't necessarily understand its philosophy or ideals. In the situations where you end up expecting something less than inspiring and some open discussions, don't give up. In Chapter 11, we will discuss the best ways to salvage those disappointing experiences.

Summary

- A School or District Edcamp or Edcamp-style event can help to provide added benefits to your next PD offering.

- Teachers love to CHOOSE what they are learning about. In the same way that we provide choice for students, we should be doing the same for educators.

- Important conversations and reflections occur when teachers have time to share.

- Educators are looking for ideas that can be implemented in the classroom immediately.

- There is value in learning from colleagues and being able to connect with them after a PD session.

- Movement and physical activity can enhance any learning experience.

Reflection Questions

How can you incorporate an Edcamp or Edcamp-style event in your own building or district? On whom could you rely to participate or help?

_____

_____

_____

_____

It's important to know your audience. How would you structure your event? Would you leave it completely open-ended with no schedule, or would you schedule some sessions?

_____

_____

_____

_____

How could you incorporate elements of Edcamp into normal PD sessions or staff meetings?

_____

_____

_____

_____

Chapter Three
Changing
the Culture

Culture eats strategy for breakfast.

—PETER DRUCKER

The most difficult thing to do in a school or school district is to change its culture. This enormous task brings to mind that famous question, "How do you eat an elephant?" The answer, of course, "One bite at a time."

Changing a school or district's culture works the same way, except that while taking one bite at a time, you must be the positive face of change at every step, modeling exactly what is expected of other educators. When I realized that my previous school district needed to change its approach to professional development, the task seemed virtually impossible to tackle. And the road was anything but smooth. When I presented my vision for personalized, relevant, and connected professional development, I received some strange (and a few angry) looks in return. Later, as we worked to implement PD content at staff meetings and create additional staff learning opportunities, I tried some things that tanked—and got a few more angry looks. But I had two things going for me: the support of my school superintendent and a monthly staff meeting with each school in the district. I knew I had to make the most of that monthly opportunity to engage our educators on a deeper level.

Bite by Bite

The good news about those monthly meetings? I got to share a consistent message with the staff members at all five of our district's school campuses. The bad news? I was sharing new ideas with staff members and challenging the status quo at all five of our district's school campuses. At first, some people were not sure what to think about my ideas for revamping PD. Sometimes my presentations fell flat. Sometimes I would ask a question and get blank stares and dead silence in return. But I kept at it.

In addition to the monthly staff meetings, which all staff members were required to attend, I started offering voluntary training sessions. On some occasions, only one person showed up. Sometimes as many as fifteen teachers attended, all eager to learn something new that would help them in their classrooms. At every meeting, I tried different strategies—some I had learned from other educators, some I simply made up—to generate stimulating conversations. (My best ideas usually came during the car ride home after particularly disappointing meetings.)

And after more than a year of hard work and dedication, things began to change. Teachers began to see that the activities might be worthwhile and that the crazy ideas just might work. They began to understand that changing how we were doing things might ultimately lead to better outcomes for students. The process of creating a culture of intentional, ongoing learning was long and included many stops and starts, but in time, those teachers and I experienced genuine professional growth.

Below are a few of the ideas I employed to add a layer of professional development to a traditional staff meeting:

Host a Problem-Solving Summit

Ask staff members to brainstorm a list of problems. Choose one or two problems that affect the majority of people in the room (or school), and collaborate on possible solutions; for example, in one school, the teachers and administrators agreed that the daily class schedule was not working. During the monthly staff meeting, we reevaluated and redesigned the school schedule. We discussed what worked and didn't work. Teachers made suggestions. I listened and took notes. We ultimately devised a new schedule to better serve the teachers' and students' needs. After running on the new schedule for several weeks, I asked for feedback. In the end, our discussion at a staff meeting led to an improved schedule, all because we used the time to fix something that wasn't working.

Host an Appy Hour

If you don't already, try moving your staff meeting to your media center. Have the media specialist select a few new apps or websites and line up teachers or even students to present each one during a staff meeting. When we tried this, the session was amazing. We limited each presenter to two minutes and then set up each one at a different station, allowing staff members to choose the apps they wanted to explore. Teachers moved excitedly from station to station, learning how to use the different tools in their classrooms. Pair your Appy Hour with three or four actual appetizers, and you'll have the winning mix for a can't-miss meeting!

Talk It Out

Teachers love to talk, especially about their passions. Why not take advantage of that passion during your next staff meeting? Set up chairs in a circle to foster discussion. (You can further encourage people to open up by having everyone do a quick share right at the opening of the meeting. Talking early tends to make people more active in the conversation throughout the meeting.) Let teachers discuss a topic like behavior management or homework. What works and doesn't work? What mistakes have led to breakthroughs in the classroom? Let teachers reflect and share resources and strategies. Allow for small-group sharing and then bring everyone back to the whole group at the end of the meeting to wrap up.

Model a Lesson

How many colleagues have you watched teach a lesson in the past year? If you're like most teachers, you simply do not have time to visit other classrooms. School leaders get to visit classrooms and see the amazing work teachers and students are doing every day, but other teachers are the ones who would benefit most from seeing their peers in action. Staff meetings can be the perfect time for peer-to-peer training—without taking up any additional time. Teachers can present a lesson to give others an idea of a method or activity that worked well in the classroom. School leaders can show they still understand what is happening in the classroom by presenting a lesson of their own. Those in the audience can do the activities and share as if they were the students, which offers tremendous insight into what students experience during a lesson.

Use Centers

Centers are a popular instructional device in the primary grades but also work well with adults during professional learning opportunities; for example, set up four centers featuring different topics and activities. Using a staff meeting this way is smart because it allows participants to stand up and move around after a long day. It also offers the freedom to direct their own learning. It is important, however, to allow for a few minutes of sharing at the end of the meeting. One way to ensure staff members visit each station is to issue them blank index cards. Have them write their name on their card and then get it stamped at each location. Then the cards with all four stamps can be placed in a box, and one card can be drawn for a modest door prize.

Throw a Picnic

Take your staff meeting outside and enjoy some fresh air at the same time by having a picnic. Ask your educators to come equipped with a blanket and one instructional strategy, resource, or idea to share with the group. Teachers can travel from blanket to blanket learning from their colleagues. If the weather doesn't cooperate, the cafeteria or gymnasium will work too. For the first twenty minutes, half of the participants walk around while the other half shares. At the twenty-minute mark, switch it up. Be sure to authenticate your picnic with actual picnic goodies to create a fun experience for the entire staff.

Dot It!

Devote a staff meeting to some professional introspection by providing your teachers a safe place to reflect on how they do their jobs. When everyone is gathered, give each teacher several dot stickers in different colors and a piece of chart paper listing various teaching practices. Assign each color a different frequency such as always, frequently, seldom, and never. Then start asking the questions and have the teachers rate themselves on their chart paper. You can ask teachers how often they use technology in the classroom, how often they use student discussion in the classroom, and how often they use questioning in the classroom. The goal is to generate discussion among the teachers as they reflect on ways to improve.

Tip Jars

Have you ever seen a trendy cafe encourage tipping by creating a debate using dueling tip jars? Steal this idea! At your next staff meeting, place two jars on a table, each labeled with a relevant workshop topic. Give each teacher a marble and let them vote on what topic they want you to present. People tend to be more willing to learn when the topic is chosen by the collective group. If the topics "win" the same number of marbles split almost down the middle, take time to learn about both topics during the meeting. I tried this at a time when my district was rolling out Google Apps for Education (now G Suite). Those of you in school districts that also went through this change know there is a huge amount of information to absorb. During one staff meeting, the jars featured labels that said "Google Drive" and "Gmail."

Most schools and districts already have staff meetings scheduled for each month. Use the monthly meeting or take a portion of it to focus on some sort of relevant professional development. This is an excellent way to promote ongoing learning, have some fun, and provide meaningful, relevant content for staff members!

Summary

- Staff meetings or voluntary meetings provide a wonderful opportunity to change the culture surrounding professional development and to add in new layers of professional learning.

- Teachers may enjoy participating in a Problem-Solving Summit, thereby getting a chance to solve some of the problems they deal with on a daily basis.

- Appy Hour provides a fun way to learn about new tech resources!

- Educators love to talk, especially when passionate about something. Give them the chance by having a discussion at your next staff meeting.

- Modeling a lesson or using centers can put instruction at the heart of your next meeting.

- Picnic PD provides a fun atmosphere for learning from colleagues.

- Dot It can provide meaningful analysis of instruction in an engaging way!

- Use Tip Jars to provide a simple choice at the beginning of each meeting.

Reflection Questions

How might you begin to change the culture surrounding professional development in your school or district?

_____

_____

_____

_____

Which of these activities can you incorporate into your next staff meeting?

_____

_____

_____

_____

How else could you switch up staff meetings in order to improve professional learning?

_____

_____

_____

_____

Chapter Four

Going ROGUE

Never doubt that a small group of thoughtful, committed, citizens can change the world. Indeed, it is the only thing that ever has.

—Margaret Mead

If you're interested in playing it safe, this might be the chapter you want to skip. We've already talked about how the notion of rethinking professional development might upset some folks. The title of this chapter could very well send some administrators into a full-blown tizzy.

"Rogue Professional Development? Who do these educators think they are? Trying to learn on their own? I won't stand for this!" said some administrator somewhere.

But try to remember what's at stake: your professional growth. If you and your colleagues are not getting the support or training that inspires continual improvement, you might need to go ROGUE, chart your own course, and make professional learning happen for yourselves.

There comes a time for every educator when they are not getting what they need. It might be a lack of support from an administrator or being forced to sit through meaningless staff meetings. It might be a lack of trust and backing from colleagues or a parent who is not able to support their child. As a teacher, I have experienced each of these situations, and I realized that if a student was not getting what he or she needed, it was my responsibility to provide it. The same applies to situations where we are not getting what we need as educators. No one else is going to take responsibility to meet our needs. We must do what we can on our own to address our own demands and wishes.

At this point, you might be wondering what it means to go ROGUE. What does it look like? What does it require? Who can do it? Is it legal? First, it's important to understand the term: R-O-G-U-E, as I am using it for the purposes of this book, is a Relevant Organized Group of Underground Educators.

A few years ago, a group of educators decided to start meeting on their own after school to continue their own learning. I was on the district's administrative team and can clearly remember the questions that arose in our meetings at the central office:

Should an administrator be there?

What will they talk about if no one is there to oversee?

What if they come up with plans that were not district approved?

What are they trying to do?

Is there any way we can stop them?

At the time, I didn't appreciate the ridiculousness of the last question. Why would we want to stop a group of committed educators who were trying to advance their own professional learning?

The answer, as some people saw it, was that this learning time and content wasn't sanctioned by the district. Those administrators worried that if teachers organized and began to learn on their own, they might "do things that we don't want them to do." There was too much that could go wrong.

Again, this kind of thinking is flawed. Instead of asking, "What could possibly go wrong?" we should have asked a more important question: "What could possibly go right?"

As they continued to meet, the group of educators asked many questions about why they had to do things a certain way. Some central office administrators continued to be angry about the questions they were asking. But a strange thing happened: Over time, teachers and administrators both realized that the meetings were ultimately having a positive impact on students in the classroom. Eventually the unsanctioned meetings led to a breakthrough in thinking, and it took a few ROGUE educators to get there. I only wish that we, as administrators, would have joined those meetings earlier and helped those students even more.

So how do you start your own ROGUE PD?

The first step is to find a group of educators who are also committed to continually pushing their professional learning boundaries. When I first connected with other educators on Twitter, I was missing something as an educator. I didn't feel supported by those who were charged with helping me to grow as a professional. I felt stifled by having my ideas shot down or minimized, and I wanted to find others who would listen to my ideas and share their own. What I found by connecting with other like-minded individuals (who were willing to challenge the status quo) completely changed my worldview. I realized that professional learning did not have to be a scheduled, sanctioned event in order to be meaningful and relevant. I found others who were changing what education and professional learning looked like, and I was forever changed by those connections.

Finding others does not have to include connecting with educators via social media. It could, but you may also go ROGUE by finding other passionate educators right in your own building or district. Know of a teacher friend who works in a different state? Perfect! Maybe your group includes other parents interested in changing the status quo. What's important here is that it doesn't matter where these like-minded individuals come from, only that they are passionate about forging their own professional learning path.

After you find others like yourself (even if it's only one or two others), the next step is to find a meeting time and place, and then spread the word. These activities can serve as the meeting focus for ROGUE Professional Development. Try any and all of these activities to help yourself and your colleagues truly grow as professionals.

Meeting of the Minds

Organize a meeting of your roguish colleagues to discuss a relevant topic. You could meet in someone's classroom before school starts to talk about what the latest brain research says about how we teach our students. You could explore the practice of assigning reading levels to students and making them pick books based on that reading level and whether that helps or hurts their progress. Really, any topic that generates thoughtful discussion and discourse is a good one. The goal should be to walk away from the meeting having been impacted by the discussion. Try to gather a varied group of educators who will bring different—even conflicting—mindsets. Remember that there is no smartest person in the room. The smartest person is the room!

Article of the Week

I know a group of thoughtful and reflective educators who felt as if they were not getting what they needed from their faculty meetings. They knew that the meetings which had started as well-intentioned had ballooned into a bloated mess of directives surrounding policies and procedures. So they formed a group that met on Fridays before school started to discuss a relevant article or blog post. One member found an item over the weekend and shared it with the group on Monday, with everyone committing to read it by the end of the week. On Friday morning, they met to debate and reflect on the article. The result? They created a simple, meaningful opportunity for genuine professional learning.

Check out
fouroclockfaculty.com
for blog posts to spark discussion.

Angry Administrator Update

Even though this was a ROGUE PD opportunity, an administrator found out about the Friday meeting, and she actually showed up. Everyone was frightened until the administrator began to share and reflect alongside the other educators. And just like the famous ending written by Dr. Seuss so many years ago in *Green Eggs & Ham*, she liked it. She really, really liked it. Now she is a regular participant in ROGUE PD.

Book Club

Gather with your group of educators to read and discuss certain books. Consider books for teachers, but also think about books that come from outside the field of education. Inspiration can be found in all kinds of places! I know a group of teachers who read the Steve Jobs biography by Walter Isaacson a few years ago. They met once a week and kept things very informal. The gathering quickly became much more of a coffee-and-friends book club than a structured professional study, and they were okay with that.

> **Need a book recommendation?** Check out *Creativity Inc.* by Ed Catmull, one of the founding partners of Pixar. It's an excellent book that can help teachers think about creativity and students.

#CoffeeEDU

Several dedicated educators have started the #CoffeeEDU movement. Anyone can host an event. The idea is pretty simple: You choose a local coffee establishment and a date and time that work, then invite other educators to join you for some rich discussion about education topics. Participants get to talk about the educational topics they choose. On any given Sunday, educators, colleagues, and friends will join at a diner or coffee shop to collaborate and share. This meet-up works well for the ROGUE learners who aren't getting what they need from their own school districts. And what could be better than meaningful discussion with dedicated educators and free coffee? Yes, you read that sentence correctly. If you are ready to host a #CoffeeEDU event, many educational vendors are willing to sponsor it so you can provide free coffee to participants. It's a win-win. Check out the hashtag on Twitter to find events that may be in your area.

Fight Club

Have you ever thought about joining up with other educators to fight?

Just kidding!

While you might be interested in physically fighting other educators, I cannot, in good conscience, promote such an activity. While a ROGUE Fight Club takes on the underground spirit of a true fight club, there's no bruising or pain involved.

Some teachers just love to argue. This is FACT. Harness that fighting spirit and invite a group of colleagues to argue debatable topics in education. The best topics are those that draw a range of emotions from participants. Maybe you debate the topic of homework: Is it beneficial or the worst thing ever created? Or standardized assessments, a topic that always brings about arguments from both sides. Try to pick an issue that elicits PASSION from both sides of the argument. When all the educators in the room feel the same way about something, the Fight Club doesn't work so well.

Because the ROGUE Fight Club *isn't* about starting a physical fight, it's smart to establish some ground rules to ensure civility.

1. **You do not talk about Fight Club.** Actually, this rule worked well for the movie, but in this case you will have to talk about the ROGUE Fight Club to promote the topic and get people excited about debating. You may want to set the expectation, however, that the debate ends when the Fight Club meeting is over—no holding grudges allowed, no impromptu arguing in the teacher's lounge the next day.

2. **This is really a debate, not a "fight."** Consider that colleagues will share their point of view on a particular subject. Attendees should feel comfortable sharing their opinions without judgment and should be prepared to defend their positions. The best arguments/discussions will be those that make people reconsider their positions. When a teacher says, "Hmmm, that is a good point. I hadn't thought of it that way," your Fight Club is successful.

3. **If it is your first time at Fight Club, you must fight.** The reason people show up to Fight Club is because they are passionate about the topic and want to share how they feel. For this reason, everyone should be encouraged to share each time they attend. Start the session by throwing out the topic and having colleagues choose sides. The pro side can move to one side of your meeting space while the con side lines up across the room.

End each ROGUE Fight Club session by having participants reflect on an argument from the other side they hadn't initially considered. This kind of reflection will help to validate the arguments of both sides and give attendees something to think about as they leave.

Underground Newsletter

Remember in high school when someone published an *underground newspaper*? The unsanctioned media source may have been created to spark controversy or to get students talking about something that the sanctioned school newspaper could not talk about. Everyone loves to get the inside scoop on things that they should

NOT be hearing about. With this in mind, consider starting an underground professional learning newsletter. Give it a cool title like this:

ROGUE PD –
Professional
Development
THEY don't want
you
to know about!

It doesn't even matter if there isn't a "they." Sharing a newsletter that colleagues might consider to be secretive, unsanctioned, or even controversial might just encourage people to read it. Share alternative resources or ideas that counter the traditional teaching that happens in your building. Use YouTube videos to convey an idea to colleagues or to show them how to use a website that no one else is using. Smore. com provides a very simple and effective way to create visually appealing newsletters that can be shared via email or social media. If you are not sure of the ramifications of sharing this type of newsletter with colleagues in your building, try it online with your PLN first.

Angry Administrator Update

Please note that unauthorized and unsanctioned professional learning opportunities, while beneficial to your own learning, might cause anxiety, stress, groans, moans, spells of anger, headaches, fits of yelling, and other as-yet-unknown symptoms to certain educational administrators. If you have not tried ROGUE PD before, please consult with a doctor first. At the very least, proceed boldly—and with extreme caution—as you attempt to improve your own professional learning.

Summary

- ROGUE Educators understand that they may have to do things on their own to get what they need.

- When going ROGUE, find a group of committed, dedicated learners who are willing to collaborate and share.

- Activities can be relatively simple. A Meeting of the Minds can center around a discussion topic, or you might gather with colleagues for an informal Book Club or to discuss the Article of the Week.

- #CoffeeEDU provides an informal opportunity to meet up with like-minded educators to talk about what's most relevant to you. It provides a way to get what YOU need.

- A Fight Club or Underground Newspaper can truly capture the underground element of finding PD about which others may not know—or want to know.

Reflection Questions

Are you getting what you need from your current staff meetings or professional learning opportunities?

_____

_____

_____

_____

Which educators would join you in exploring ROGUE learning?

_____

_____

_____

_____

How can you incorporate ROGUE activities into your current PD experiences?

_____

_____

_____

_____

Chapter Five
Making Every Minute Count

Time is what we want most,
but what we use worst.

—WILLIAM PENN

The moment the instructor asked the question, I knew she would get a painfully honest answer. I was sitting in on a training session for a new math program. Some of the teachers in attendance said they were not making it through each math lesson on a daily basis. They were running out of time and leaving required activities unfinished. The instructor, who was not only a content and curriculum specialist but also a seasoned teacher, replied to the teachers' frustration with one simple question, "How much time out of your fifty-minute math lesson do you actually have to teach math?" Without missing a beat, one teacher answered, "We have forty-one-and-a half minutes. We lose two minutes to the students entering the classroom, two more minutes to them exiting the classroom, then two more to taking attendance. We lose another two minutes to handing in homework, and thirty seconds to getting their attention to start the math lesson."

Clearly the teacher had a very good handle on numbers. And perhaps we could tweak some of her classroom-management issues to improve the efficiency of the math lessons. But the real issue for this educator and for teachers, instructional aides, and administrators everywhere is that we are all constantly battling the sands of time.

Time is at a premium for every educator. Think about your own struggles with "getting it all done." There's a never-ending list of things to do:

> I have a forty-minute prep period. Should I grade the writing papers and provide feedback for students, or should I prepare for tomorrow's science experiment?

> How am I going to finish report cards and prepare meaningful discussion points for parent conferences?

> When will I have a chance to reteach struggling learners after I lost twenty minutes to a fire drill this morning?

> How am I ever going to fit a fifty-minute lesson into forty-one-and-a-half minutes?

I have been in education for approximately fifteen years, and I can tell you from experience that there is never enough time in the day. Today's technology makes some tasks faster, but teachers also have more daily responsibilities than ever before.

So when I hear frustration and opposition when I propose that educators are responsible for growing professionally, I get it. Professional development can seem like one more item on an already too-long to-do list. The question isn't whether it is important to find time to learn something that will make us better educators. Of course it's important, just like many of the items that are on our to-do list. The real question is, where do we find the time for PD in our already busy days?

We will never have a surplus of time, but if we look at our daily schedules and find ways to maximize the spare minutes we do have, we can ensure PD time becomes meaningful and relevant. Start by looking at your daily schedule. How much time can you conceivably use for your own professional learning? Go ahead, take a minute and map out your day. What time is available to you to learn something that will help you move forward as an educator? The time is probably limited to your daily prep period, your lunch period, and a few minutes before or after school.

Some schools and districts make professional learning a priority by sending students home early one afternoon a month. The teachers then have ninety minutes to two hours to dedicate to professional development. In one of my previous districts, we shortened the school days during the first and last weeks of school to provide ninety minutes of professional-learning time each afternoon for teachers to focus on learning new initiatives or programs, try out new computer programs or websites, or simply plan or reflect.

Not every school or district is able (or willing) to offer this dedicated time to teachers for PD on a regular basis. Regardless of how much time your school or district allots for learning, planning, and reflection, there are a few strategies and activities you can use to capture the time you do have and make it count.

Lunch and Learn

Lunchtime is a perfect time for professional development. The only thing I love more than learning something new is learning something new while eating. Can you relate? Whether you have a twenty-minute break or a full forty-minute period for lunch, choose to use that time productively.

Here's how Lunch and Learn works: First, figure out the food. It might sound silly, but it's critical to get that right. Lunchtime is a valuable commodity for teachers, and some days it's the only downtime you'll have. If you're on a tight budget, a BYOB—Bring Your Own Bag—works nicely. If you have some money to play with, quick and easy options like pizza, sub sandwiches, or bagels and cream cheese are perfect. Then invite a few of your colleagues to your Lunch and Learn. Let them know about the food arrangements and what the topic will be. You could choose to discuss a new educational app or website or a trending instructional strategy. Or you could tackle an issue that is sure to spark discussion. Keep in mind, the best professional development sessions often start with a question.

List Your Learning

Set up a whiteboard in the faculty room or other key area where teachers are known to gather. Another option is to cover a table or wall with dry-erase paint. This type of paint is common in many paint stores, and covers a surface with a white paint on which you can write with dry erase markers. Post questions or instructional strategies for teachers, and allow them to add their own ideas or strategies. I use a small whiteboard next to our teacher sign-in, and I post a daily message. Sometimes I write an inspirational quote or message. Sometimes I pose a question or list a website or instructional strategy. Last week,

I left copies of a questioning grid next to the daily message where I wrote "Take one" and drew an arrow. It's a simple routine, but the clear message is that professional learning is important. In fact, when I'm late with the message in the morning, teachers will return later in the day to see what I've written.

#TechMex Tuesday

One of the more successful professional development offerings I have used in the past is #TechMexTuesday. It combines the idea of Tech Tuesday and Taco Tuesday (*LEGO Movie* fans unite!) for a fun new twist. I suggest implementing #TechMexTuesday during those underutilized pockets of time just before school starts and just after it ends. The concept is simple: In the ten to fifteen minutes teachers are required to be in the building—either before students arrive or after they leave—invite them to learn about some kind of new technology and snack on some grab-and-go Tex-Mex treats. This may seem like a short amount of time, but fifteen minutes gives you the opportunity to share something worthwhile. Some educators may stay beyond the allotted time to further explore the concept or resource, while others may leave to explore on their own.

After the success of #TechMexTuesday in our school, we expanded the concept to the summer months. We hosted a half-hour session each Tuesday featuring a new tech resource or instructional strategy, then left a half-hour for exploration. Those in attendance loved it! We even had educators come from other districts, and long-distance connections were made. While summer vacation is the most precious of timeframes for educators, many educators are looking for professional learning opportunities during this time. Even if educators are using this much-needed time off to recharge and reenergize for the following school year, they might still love to continue learning throughout the summer.

Five-Minute PD

Another idea with which I have experimented is finding even shorter timeframes to expand teacher knowledge. With even five extra minutes, teachers can learn about a new resource or strategy to incorporate into their classrooms. When my district started implementing Google Apps for Education a few years ago, we wanted to provide teachers with a quick resource to help guide them. We sent out five-minute videos that explained how to use a particular feature or perform a certain function. What was great about the videos was that staff members could watch them again and again until they were able to utilize the tool. Offering up quick-hitting PD gives teachers the chance to quickly learn how to utilize a particular function of interactive projector software or even take a few minutes to explore a new website. Every little minute counts, and these informal sessions provided teachers with the support they needed to be successful.

1-5-15

Rob Sahli, an assistant principal in Minnesota, was seeking a way for his staff members to utilize available time to continue learning. Each week, Rob shares the 1-5-15 Bulletin. Each edition, created through Smore.com, features three links that help educators continue their learning. The first link takes approximately one minute to review, the second link only five minutes, and the third link takes just about fifteen minutes. Rob's hope is that with just a few minutes, the content of the bulletin will have an impact on the teachers and their classrooms. With ever shorter timeframes to devote to professional learning, ideas like the 1-5-15 Bulletin can help inspire educators to continue learning.

#PopUpPD

If you have never heard of a Pop Up Shop or a Pop Up Restaurant, it is a store or restaurant that is opened in a temporary space for a limited length of time. It may often coincide with a cultural event or happening; for example, we might see Pop Up Shops opening during the Olympics or World Cup.

Professional Development is also something that should be happening anytime and anywhere. This is where #PopUpPD comes into play. Think about a great topic or question that may generate some great professional discourse. Write down the topic or question on a piece of paper and post it in the main office (where teachers sign in) or in the faculty room. Invite teachers to discuss, learn, and share, and to post their answers in a specific spot. You might leave sticky notes for colleagues to share resources, or you might ask them to share via a hashtag on social media (more on this in Chapter 6).

> Check out fouroclockfaculty.com for printable #PopUpPD topics and questions you can easily share with colleagues.

Keep It Simple—Make It Fun

As you're thinking about using those fifteen minutes after school when everyone is still in the building, remember that PD can be fun! At one after-school session last year, I shared a website called Geoguessr. This game site places players at some mystery location somewhere in the world. By exploring the area using Google Maps, players look for clues, using critical thinking and deductive reasoning skills to eventually guess the mystery location. When I showed the staff, the fifteen-minute session turned into an hour-long session, as the staff played the addictive game well beyond when I thought they would! The best part of hosting this particular session was that classrooms were abuzz the next day with students using those same critical thinking skills alongside teachers as they played the game together. Sometimes it's the simple professional-learning activities that can have the most impact on the classroom.

Microlearning

I spend a lot of my time hanging out in a Dojo. I wish I could say that I am becoming a master of the martial arts, but I'm mostly watching as my children learn many skills that I hope will help them later on in life: hard work, determination, commitment to a goal, and how *not* to get hit during dodgeball at the end of class. As I've sat and watched, however, I've learned something about learning.

The owner and head of the gym also teaches the children's classes. In a forty-five-minute session, he runs the students through twelve to fifteen activities. Each activity starts with a quick round of modeling followed by a quick round of guided and independent practice, and then the class moves on to the next activity. Many of the skills are repeated from class to class, and the repetition in short bursts helps the kids to master the skills.

This type of microlearning can work in a professional development setting as well. Microlearning, by definition, should be short. Once a week, host a microlearning opportunity. Think ten to fifteen minutes before or after school: for example, share a two-minute video on creativity in the classroom, and ask a follow-up question. Have colleagues discuss the question for two minutes, and ask how this might impact their instruction tomorrow. Or gather colleagues and spend five to ten minutes writing down all of the higher-order thinking questions you would like to ask students during the next week. Then share the questions.

Microlearning PD should allow the participants to learn about and practice skills that will help them become better educators. Stuck for ideas for your next microlearning section? Check out *fouroclock-faculty.com* for some great resources. Each microlearning video presents some great strategies and resources for teachers in a short video and ends with a call to action—a task that the viewer should complete following the video. These resources are perfect for microlearning opportunities in your professional setting.

Summary

- There will never be enough time in the day, especially for educators. Finding available time to complete meaningful PD can be difficult but ultimately rewarding.

- Lunch & Learn is the perfect opportunity for educators to gather, learn, and share while also enjoying a great meal.

- A simple PD message or resource posted each morning in the Faculty Room or Main Office can set the tone for the day!

- Educators love learning and eating at the same time! Try #TechMexTuesday to provide great technology resources while serving up some Tex-Mex Grab-and-Go.

- Activities that educators can do in five to ten minutes work well for professional learning. Try Five-Minute PD, a 1-5-15 Bulletin, Microlearning, or #PopUpPD to encourage staff and colleagues to continue learning!

- Most of all, keep it simple and make it fun to take advantage of the minutes available each day for meaningful Professional Development.

Reflection Questions

Where can you find a few extra minutes in your day to incorporate short PD opportunities? What are you doing that may not be a valuable use of your time?

_____

_____

_____

_____

Which PD activities can you implement with some of your colleagues that take advantage of your available time?

_____

_____

_____

_____

What resources, strategies, or websites can you share with colleagues in a short amount of time?

_____

_____

_____

_____

Chapter Six
Taking Advantage of Twitter

*The problem with quotes on the Internet
is that they are often not true.*

—ABRAHAM LINCOLN (NOT VERIFIED)

$\mathscr{P}$icture the scene: You're sitting on your couch in the most comfortable pair of pajamas you own and eating a giant bowl of rocky road ice cream topped with hot fudge and whipped cream. In fact, it's dark chocolate hot fudge because you know dark chocolate is a healthier option. You settle in for the next hour, but you're not getting ready to watch your favorite television show or the latest Hollywood blockbuster. You're about to immerse yourself in a Twitter chat and learn assessment techniques to use with your students tomorrow. These techniques will be shared by other expert educators from around the world who also might be sitting in their own living rooms, in their own comfy pajamas and with their own dessert of choice.

There was a time when such a professional-development opportunity wasn't possible or even imaginable. But today we live in a world where it happens all the time. Educators can learn anytime, anywhere—even from the comfort of their own home.

The biggest factor that has changed how all of us learn is a tool that some educators are still unwilling to use or are not quite sure about. I fell into social media a few short years ago. I had learned about Twitter at a conference session I attended. I found out that there were other educators out there sharing their ideas with the world. Good ideas. My connection through Twitter was gradual. Whenever I was getting ready to host a staff meeting, I would peruse Twitter to look for some new ideas. Every few weeks I would jump on to see what was shared. Then I discovered Twitter chats, where other educators would gather at a specific time to share about a specific topic. Over time I became a regular, and it has made all the difference.

Discovering Twitter changed my worldview on what is possible in education. The number of great educators who share and reflect upon their own learning has inspired me to no end. On Twitter, I have had the opportunity to connect and share with educators from all over the world and to bring that learning back to my own roles in education.

If you aren't already on Twitter, take five minutes to create a profile today. If you are already taking advantage of the connections and chats happening on Twitter, spread the word! Whether you are leading a ROGUE PD meetup or hosting "sanctioned" PD sessions, devote some time to showing teachers the power of the Twitterverse. Create opportunities for teachers to share and reflect upon their learning, find resources, or connect with educational leaders near and far. I am convinced that Twitter offers some of the best PD opportunities, and it's available 24/7. It's on-demand professional learning at its finest. Here are a few ways you can jump in. (Be sure to bring a few colleagues with you.)

Host a Book Study

A few years ago, as I was trying to change the culture surrounding professional learning, I decided teachers could learn as much as I could if they would just join Twitter. The problem was that no one was readily joining Twitter on their own. I needed something to entice them. I wanted to host a district-wide book club for staff, but several logistical problems held us back. Each of the five schools in our district ran on different schedules, which meant teachers started and finished their day at different times. Any time I chose for a face-to-face meeting would leave some teachers sitting around waiting for the meeting or cause some teachers to show up late. The solution to this problem was to host the book study as a Twitter chat.

Of the approximately thirty teachers who volunteered to participate in the book study, about a third had used Twitter previously and felt comfortable with posting and sharing. Another third had signed up for accounts at some point but never used Twitter, and the remaining members of the group had no experience with Twitter prior to our book study. So I offered a face-to-face meeting for educators who were new to Twitter so they could set up their profiles and learn the basics about using the social media platform. We simulated a brief chat so everyone could see how the questions would post and how to respond within a chat on Twitter. Also at this first meeting, we voted on a time that would work for everyone and chose our first book. We chose *Teach Like A PIRATE*.

Every Monday night, our group of thirty committed educators joined to discuss the book. We talked about engagement strategies, bringing passion to the classroom, and ultimately, how to transform our classrooms. The group of teachers ranged from Pre-K teachers who found some insight into how they could impact even their classroom to technology educators who discovered new tools and strategies for engaging students. The best part of hosting a book study through a Twitter chat was that the author himself was able to join in and share with our teachers. We felt as if we were meeting a celebrity.

Join a #Chat

Post a question for discussion and share answers throughout the day or week. Traditional educational chats on Twitter have taken on a life of their own. Participants connect on Twitter at a set time, say Monday, 9 p.m., on a particular hashtag (#tlap), and everyone shares their expertise or questions.

One particular type of chat, the slow Edchat, can also be beneficial. In this type of chat, a question is posted using a specific hashtag, and participants share their responses throughout the day or week. This allows all participants to share when they are able, and they don't have to be on Twitter at a specific time.

Create a District or School PD Hashtag

Many schools or districts create their own hashtag to share resources or strategies. This allows staff members to share any great Tweets they may stumble across; for example, if you find a great social studies resource that you think might benefit your colleagues, you can share that resource using your school PD hashtag. You could also share at existing hashtags that might be relevant, such as #TechTuesday, #4OCF, #RevolutionizePD, or #ProfDev.

Scavenger Hunt

Have teachers search for and find valuable resources. This can be an awesome way to add some fun at your school and challenge colleagues to find and share excellent resources. Create a list of things that teachers must find. Ideas might include…

1. Find and share a great science website.
2. Find and share digital citizenship resources.
3. Find and share an excellent math lesson for teaching geometry.
4. Find and share self-care resources for teachers.
5. Find and share a blog with great resources for teachers, such as fouroclockfaculty.com.

After teachers find these things, they get to share them via Twitter using a hashtag, something like *#YourSchool*ScavengerHunt. Have colleagues pair up or join a team, and see who can check off the most items on the scavenger hunt list or who can complete the entire list in the shortest amount of time.

This idea could work as part of a staff meeting, or educators can log on to Twitter on their own time to share their found scavenger hunt resources. Chances are that most participants will share different resources to check off each item on the list. At the end of the scavenger hunt, you and your colleagues will have a wealth of resources at your fingertips to help improve learning for you and your students.

Explore the Virtues of Voxer

In addition to Twitter, other social apps can be utilized to continue your learning. The ***Voxer*** app is perfect for teachers who are looking to connect and go beyond the 140 characters of Twitter. Voxer allows teachers to leave messages for each other. The walkie-talkie-type app allows anyone to leave a message for someone or for a group of people at any time. You can use it to create conversations between grade-level teams, as a forum for a book study, or to connect your teachers with experts in the field. The app gives teachers the chance to talk, collaborate, share, and discuss. This allows for asynchronous communication for educators. What's great about the messaging tool is that communication via voice messages allows for more context than simple text messages or Twitter posts. You can also share text messages, links, photos, and resources.

I first learned about Voxer at an Edcamp a few years ago. Intrigued, I listened to educators explain the app and how it expanded the power of Twitter by allowing for actual discussions to take place. From the moment I tried it, I was instantly hooked.

When I first became an administrator, I came from a background in teaching math and science.

As a curriculum supervisor, I also needed to become an expert in literacy instruction. I turned to Voxer and joined the #g2great group. This group chats each week on Twitter, but extends the conversations on Voxer. Participating in this group by sharing, reflecting on my own practice, and asking questions allowed me to learn more about literacy instruction. The Voxer app—like Twitter and other tech-connected media—proves that collective knowledge is greater than that of one individual.

Many of the same strategies that we just talked about for Twitter can be applied using Voxer. Questions of the Day work particularly well with it. Last year we took our book study to Voxer, eliminating the need for teachers to gather online at the same time. Teachers were able to leave voice responses to questions and generate discussion on their own time, creating a way for nonparallel communication. For the book study, I recorded a voice message for each question, and teachers responded at their convenience. Teachers needed some time to adjust to sharing recorded messages (typing words in a Twitter chat is a different experience than recording yourself talking about something), but ultimately they were able to share valuable insight utilizing the tool.

Angry Administrator Update

When I talk about the power of Twitter or other forms of social media as professional development, administrators often ask me whether teachers deserve continuing education hours credit for that type of learning. Some administrators say that because they can't verify whether someone participated in a chat, they cannot award professional development credit for the time teachers spend learning outside a supervised setting. For all the grumpy administrators who might feel this way, I will let you in on a little secret: The educators who are out there learning on their own don't really care about the credit. They are in it for the learning. For the record, however, I did award credit for the time educators spent learning when they would complete a professional-development activity using the Twitter platform. It was very easy to verify by simply documenting their tweets or sharing what teachers did. Most importantly, I believed they deserved it.

Summary

- Twitter can serve as an on-demand professional development resource for educators.

- A book study is a great way to draw educators into Twitter. Choose a book and a hashtag, and share your book reflections with colleagues via Twitter.

- Starting a district or school PD hashtag allows educators to share and easily find resources with one another.

- Scavenger Hunts, Question(s) of the Day, and Chats provide additional opportunities to connect with other educators to improve your practice.

- Voxer is a great app that allows you to go beyond Twitter to connect and exchange voice messages for other dedicated professionals.

Reflection Questions

If you have not joined Twitter yet, what is holding you back? Is there another educator you know who uses Twitter who can help show you the basics?

_____

_____

_____

_____

If you are already on Twitter, how can you help spread the word about the benefits? What activities could you lead that might draw other educators onto Twitter?

_____

_____

_____

_____

How can you use Voxer or other social media to help improve your own professional learning?

_____

_____

_____

_____

Chapter Seven

Going It Alone

*It's better to be alone than
in bad company.*

—GEORGE WASHINGTON

We have spent a great deal of time talking about connecting with other educators who are as passionate as you. Sharing, connecting, and learning from others is an important step in the right direction to improving your own professional learning. But sometimes we all need a little alone time. There are times when you need to disconnect from others, to reflect on your own, to spend time doing something for yourself. Be willing to go it alone. It's going to be okay. Trust me: You can learn a lot all by yourself. In fact, one of the most important things any of us can do for our professional learning is to carve out time alone to think and reflect in order to improve.

Let's imagine that you are the only teacher in your building teaching a particular subject or grade level. Maybe you are the only art or music teacher. Maybe you are a department of one at the high school level. Maybe you teach at a very small school and are the only second grade teacher. While it may seem lonely at times, I encourage you to embrace your isolation. There are plenty of things you can do, all by yourself, to continue to learn.

Here are a few ways to make the most of moments of isolation or other alone time you find throughout the course of a given week:

Embrace the Morning

Every morning, about an hour before the rest of my family wakes up, I get up and spend some time in personal reflection. I think about what my day will bring and about ideas or concerns I have been trying to process. I might jot down a checklist to make sure that I accomplish my major goals for the day. On some mornings, I'll spend fifteen to twenty minutes writing, documenting my thoughts and drafting what later become blog posts. It gets the creative juices flowing and starts my day with my head in the right space.

Extend Your Evenings

Each night I usually extend my evening by finding some time to read. For twenty to thirty minutes right before bed, I'll read a book, journal article, or blog posts. This time allows me to find solutions to problems I might be facing or find new ideas to implement to improve learning outcomes for students and teachers.

Enjoy a Quiet Lunch

As a teacher, I ate lunch in the faculty lunchroom with colleagues on most days. But once a week, I ate lunch alone in my classroom. This time alone allowed me to think about how the morning lessons had gone, which students still needed help, and how I could arrange the afternoon's lessons to meet student needs. While I missed the camaraderie of the lunchroom, the additional quiet time was a nice, peaceful gift.

Decompress on Fridays

During my teaching career, one of my favorite times was Friday afternoon. Students would be on the bus by 3:25 p.m., and I would be back in my classroom by 3:30 p.m., enjoying the quiet and reflecting on the week. I usually spent thirty minutes to an hour considering which lessons had worked or not worked, what skills and objectives students still needed to master, and how to improve learning outcomes in the week to come. The time spent quietly in the classroom on Friday afternoons allowed me to clear my mind to better enjoy the weekend and re-energize for the next school week.

Commute with Care

For several years, my commute to work took a little more than an hour each way. While you may not have such a lengthy commute, whatever time you do have can be used to think and learn. This is a great time to listen to podcasts. Some of my favorites are PodcastPD, My Bad, Revisionist History, Why I Write, and The Moment with Brian Koppelman.

The time spent commuting can also give you an opportunity to weigh and propose options that might help you accomplish something later in the day or the next day. I find some of my best ideas while I am driving. Using my smartphone's notetaking app allows me to capture those ideas.

The drive home can be an especially important reflection time. My current commute is about forty-five minutes. I use this time to mentally unpack my day. I try to reflect on what went well, what could have gone better, and what I need to work on for the next day. Dedicating this time to reflection (and recording my thoughts and ideas with my smartphone) allows me to quiet my brain by the time I pull in my driveway. I am then able to dedicate more of myself to my family.

Time spent in isolation can do wonders for the soul and even inspire the time spent connecting and collaborating with others. Back in 1956, Walt Disney gave an interview in which he talked about plussing his theme park, Disneyland. The idea was to constantly tinker to improve and grow what was possible in his theme park. Walt stressed the idea of plussing with his imagineers, often asking them to "plus" their ideas, to constantly make them better. How can you use your alone time to plus your professional learning? Students need you to become a better learner in order to become better learners themselves. Try these PPL (Plussed Professional Learning) ideas to improve learning for your students:

Learn Something New

Each week, try to learn one new thing that will help your students. It doesn't matter what it is. You might research how teaching empathy can help to improve the climate and culture in your classroom. You might dedicate yourself to learning more about how digital citizenship skills can be infused across the curriculum. If you want to connect with students, find out what the latest app is that your students are using, and spend the week learning about it and trying it out. Chances are they'll be on to the next big thing by the next week, but you will have learned something new.

Spend Ten Minutes a Day on Twitter

Set a timer and step boldly into the Twitterverse. You could use the time to seek new instructional strategies or connect with experts in the field of content that you or your students are currently exploring. A few years ago, while researching creativity in the classroom, I reached out to several thought leaders outside of education to get their opinion on the topic. I sent out a couple of tweets to these people and was shocked when I received helpful replies. Lee Cockerell, the former head of the Disney Resorts, even sent information about how Disney encourages creativity and innovation among its cast members. By spending just a few minutes on Twitter, I was able to connect with someone who has spent years innovating for Disney. Whether it's sharing with your local colleagues, participating in a Twitter chat, or connecting with experts across the country, Twitter can make a powerful daily impact on your professional learning.

Spend Time Reflecting Each Day

If there is a single act that educators can do each day that will help them improve, it is building in the practice of reflection. Spending even a few minutes a day looking back at your recent successes and failures can help you to move forward and progress on a daily basis. Try these questions to help you reflect each day:

- What went well today?
- What can I improve upon tomorrow?
- How did I make a difference for someone today?
- What did I learn today?

- How did it change my thinking?
- What kind of impact did I have?

If you can answer each of these questions, you will not only become a better educator, but also a better learner and a better person. These reflective practice questions will help you to improve in all of your roles and ensure that you are becoming an educator who ultimately impacts students.

Execute a Brilliant or Not-So-Brilliant Idea Each Week!

There is something about the early morning hours that allows me to come up with my best ideas. It might be while I'm in the shower or when I'm sitting at a dimly lit desk trying to write while not waking anyone else up. Sometimes the ideas work. Many times they don't. But to find out, they must be executed. Each week I try out one of these ideas.

For example, several weeks ago I had the brilliant idea of turning our school cafeteria into the Great Hall of Hogwarts. You see, our lunches had become a little unruly, and I was looking for something that could help with student behavior when I stumbled upon a Harry Potter marathon on TV. I was inspired by the regal environment in the Great Hall and decided that this would be the perfect backdrop for our students in the cafeteria. We had a sorting ceremony, complete with a sorting hat, which assigned students to one of the Hogwarts houses. Banners with each of the house logos were hung in the cafeteria. Majestic music was played, and my dramatic side, if you want to call it that, made a brief appearance. I completely expected this would help to improve behavior for the students while they ate lunch. I hoped that the students would feel a sense of belonging to one of the houses, and therefore would better meet expectations in the cafeteria. As I reflected a few weeks later, I was trying to figure out why it was a dud—in terms of ways to improve lunchtime behavior. Student behavior did not improve. In fact, the competitive nature made it worse. I believe that in my haste to implement such a plan, I had not provided students with enough time or motivation to buy in, and I had not explained how this new structure could help everyone in the cafeteria. The good news is that I think the idea is salvageable with some tweaks to presentation, format, structure, and perhaps a better actor. Don't be afraid to try out new ideas. It's the only way we progress through life.

Executing ideas related to your own professional learning each week can be relatively easy. Try out any of the ideas in the book, or come up with a new idea to improve learning for yourself or your colleagues. In fact, let's commit to a little action research right now. If you are currently at school and reading this book, put down the book (especially if you are supposed to be doing something else). Find five people and ask them a *Why do we...* question.

- Why do we assign thirty math problems for homework?
- Why do we only meet once or twice a month as a staff?
- Why do we give students extra credit for things that their parents should be doing?
- Why do we group students according to age rather than need?
- Why do we assume that tasks can be accomplished in forty-five-minute chunks of time?
- Why do we often assign students with the most needs to teachers with the least experience?

If you are not reading the book at school right now, then come up with your *Why do we...* question and be prepared to ask five people the next time you are in school. I promise you it will generate some interesting discussion. You may get some curt responses or some weird looks, but it will definitely get people thinking. If you are feeling really adventurous, expand the circle of people that you ask. Go from five to twenty-five.

See how easy it is to execute new ideas? Even if this idea failed, you at least know how some people feel about homework.

There are inevitably going to be times when you are working alone. Don't be discouraged by this alone time or professional isolation. The key is to use this time creatively, to innovate on your own, and, after YOU come up with a good idea, to share it. Remember that the time spent learning, thinking, and reflecting alone can help to improve the time spent collaborating with others. As you will see in our next section, professional development time can help you to go beyond learning as you focus on creation, problem solving, and even redefining what is possible when you engage in professional learning.

Summary

- Being alone or isolated as an educator can provide the necessary time to reflect and grow as an individual.

- Carve out some alone time to sit back, think, and contemplate. Whether it's waking up early, staying up late, eating lunch by yourself, or reflecting during your commute, find the time that is right for you.

- Whenever you find your time, be sure to reflect each day. Try asking a series of reflection questions that will help you improve and grow as a learner.

- Find time to commit to executing a brilliant or not-so-brilliant idea each week. If you learn about something new, try it with students. The only way to improve is to try and fail—and learn from your mistakes.

Reflection Questions

When can you find alone time to reflect or grow as a learner? What time works best for you?

_____

_____

_____

_____

How can you use time in isolation to improve professional learning?

_____

_____

_____

_____

What brilliant ideas can you try to implement? How will you reflect on the implementation?

_____

_____

_____

_____

Section 3

Beyond Learning

Chapter Eight

Solving Problems

> *We cannot solve our problems*
> *with the same thinking we*
> *used when we created them.*
>
> —Albert Einstein

Quick. Answer the following question. Don't think about it. Just shout out an answer—unless you're sitting near people who wouldn't appreciate such an outburst.

Ready? Here we go: What is the most rewarding professional development experience you've ever had?

Chances are a particular session or workshop probably comes to mind. Maybe the session you thought of left you inspired and motivated to return to your classroom. Maybe you learned about a great technology resource that you could add to your repertoire to engage students. Maybe you connected with like-minded educators to work collaboratively on a project for your students.

For me, the best professional learning sessions were sessions that helped me solve a problem. Earlier in the book, I talked about how I was surprised the first time I heard of teachers actually calling in sick on a professional development day. It was that very problem I was struggling to solve when I found myself attending my first Edcamp. I was inspired and motivated and encouraged by the amazing atmosphere, but most importantly, that workshop helped me find a workable solution I could take back home to my district. I knew that once teachers saw the power of the collaborative, conversational style of the unconference model, they would be more willing to participate and less likely to find other (less meaningful) ventures to fill their professional learning time.

Chris Sacca is a venture capitalist and investor who has invested in and been involved in the early stages of companies like Twitter, Uber, Instagram, and Kickstarter. More importantly, he has reached the pinnacle of success by appearing as an investor on one of my children's favorite television shows, *Shark Tank*. While listening to Chris being interviewed on a podcast recently, I was intrigued when he talked about how he and his friends would gather at his house late at night, order some food, and host a jam session. The purpose was to talk through ideas and discuss and solve problems they were dealing with at the time. As I listened, I realized that we don't do nearly enough of this in education. As educators, our plates are full of puzzles, challenges, and obstacles. Wouldn't it be great to have someone take one of those issues off your plate and match it up with a solution? Of course it would—but I suspect it's up to you and me and other like-minded colleagues to make it happen.

A huge part of problem solving is taking a leap into the unknown, so I say go for it. Gather a few of your colleagues—rogues or otherwise—and host a jam session, either at school or another comfortable setting where you can talk freely. I suggest following these five steps to get your jam sessions going:

1. **Choose five problems to solve.** When I say "problems," I mean areas where concrete changes or improvements can be made. It might be helpful to solicit a few ideas from colleagues prior to the meeting, or you could make that the first task of the jam session. A few universal problems include improving collaboration in math class, making writing tasks more authentic, making schedules work better for students, and reaching reluctant learners.

2. **Have participants choose which problem they want to solve.** The division of labor can be decided prior to the jam session to save time, or you can break into groups at the last minute. Either way, make sure the problems you are tackling are meaningful problems that everyone in the jam session encounters with some regularity.

3. **Allow twenty-five minutes of discussion, debate, and sharing.** Convey that no idea is a bad idea, and establish a no-judgment zone. Keep in mind that what might work for one person might not work for another. Some disagreement during the discussion is healthy, so let all the participants speak their minds. Keep a running list of problems and their corresponding solutions.

4. **Set aside fifteen minutes for reflection.** At this point, participants should be able to leave the jam session armed with multiple solutions they plan to utilize in the classroom; for example, if your daily mini-lesson, which is supposed to be no longer than five to ten minutes, keeps swallowing up half (or worse, *all*) of your class period, a simple solution could

be using a timer. A simple kitchen timer works well, or you can find a timer online. Set it for five minutes, and when the buzzer goes off, move on with your lesson.

5. **Distribute all of the groups' solutions to all participants via email.** In addition, provide time at a subsequent meeting to evaluate how things went and which solutions were more successful than others, and why.

That's it—five steps. Can you host a jam session tomorrow with some of your colleagues? Absolutely! You might want to approach an administrator about hosting a session at your next faculty meeting. If you can't find enough committed educators in your building or district, try reaching out to educators in your Professional Learning Network. Follow Chris Sacca's lead. Order some food, sit down with the brightest people you know, and figure out a solution to a problem that you deal with every day.

Angry Administrator Update

Even if you come up with the best solution to an ongoing problem that your students are facing, some administrators might not be willing or able to implement your solution right away, if at all. Don't give up. Talk with the administrator about why the solution makes the most sense. If there are obstacles to implementing the solution, help the administrator figure out how to eliminate the obstacles or work around them. Don't forget, you are a problem solver.

Summary

- Every educator has specific challenges, problems, and issues that they deal with every day. Yet we rarely take time to solve these problems.

- A Jam Session can offer the opportunity for you and your colleagues to identify the problems you are dealing with and solve them in a structured format.

- Set aside time at a faculty meeting, or find colleagues who might be experiencing the same problems as you. Once you identify a problem, remember that no solution is a bad solution as long as it fixes the problem.

Reflection Questions

What are some problems or challenges you face each day?
How do these problems impact your day?

_____

_____

_____

_____

Which colleagues might be experiencing the same
difficulties? With whom would you be willing to partner to
host a Jam Session?

_____

_____

_____

_____

How might you generate possible solutions to your
problems? What resources can you use to help solve your
problems?

_____

_____

_____

_____

Chapter Nine
Creating Something Meaningful

*A year from now, you may wish
you had started today.*

—KAREN LAMB

I f you are a fan of *Four O'Clock Faculty*, you might have read our first-ever post. It details the origins of the Four O'Clock Faculty (#4OCF). Although the blog was an idea I had entertained for well over a year, I had trouble taking the first step. Then came one of my most important professional learning experiences ever—a snow day!

That's right, as the snow fell on that cold day in January, I lounged in my PJs, sipped hot chocolate, and finally started writing. I wrote the two posts that ultimately led to the website. Since then I have truly evolved as an educator. The #4OCF platform has provided me with amazing connections, the ability to write candidly about public education, and countless opportunities to perfect my skills and reflect on my own professional growth. To some, that snow day might not be all that memorable, but for me it was something of a turning point in my life. And why not? We have established that professional growth can and should be happening anywhere, at any time. Sometimes it takes the form of problem solving. Other times professional development is about educators simply taking the time to create. Imagine a day—or even a few hours—of professional development during which your only directive is to create something new or beautiful or useful or fun. What would you do? What would you create?

This kind of professional development does exist, but it's a bit of a hard sell in some school districts. Not everyone gets it. Not everyone sees the value in flexing those creative muscles. I do, and I believe we need to do more of it. Here are a few ways to inject some creativity into your professional development sessions:

Genius Hour

Many teachers have experimented with Genius Hour or 20% Time projects with students. The idea originated with Google where employees were encouraged to devote up to 20 percent of their work time to innovation. Although the projects explored during this time didn't necessarily relate to employees' regular roles and tasks, much of what happened in those hours led to innovations that helped push Google forward. In the classroom, setting aside a Genius Hour provides both teachers and students an opportunity to embrace their passions and interests. Perhaps you have been looking to incorporate design thinking into a science unit. Genius Hour is the time to do it. Maybe you want to start a geocaching club to teach real-world and real-time geography skills. Here's your answer. The logistics are relatively simple. Schedule a Genius Hour for your next staff meeting. Allow your school's educators to engage in whatever activities they find stimulating and challenging. The only rule? The work they choose must directly benefit students.

FedEx Day

I believe that most teachers, after having the experience of using professional learning time to create something meaningful, will want to take this model to the next level. In his book *Drive*, author Daniel Pink examines the idea of "FedEx Day." This day began in some businesses as a twenty-four-hour session of creation. Employees were encouraged to use the time to work on anything they wanted as long as they shared what they had created with colleagues twenty-four hours later, delivering overnight just like FedEx. Very clever. Many school districts have adopted this practice, and it can provide for meaningful creation. I believe it has immense potential.

Consider what might happen if a few teachers at your school sat down with the school counselor and brainstormed a few ways to reinvigorate the Positive Behavioral Support System. Or what if one teacher used that time to create a newsletter for parents that could be shared with all his or her grade-level counterparts? Or imagine your school's physical education teachers organizing a Ninja warrior-style obstacle course that teachers could utilize before school and students could use throughout the day. The possibilities for creation are endless! My advice is to resist the urge to focus on what might go wrong and instead dream about all that could go right. And then start creating! The results might surprise you.

Blogging

When people ask me why I blog, my answer is a simple one, but I'm not sure everyone understands: I blog for myself. Although writing for *Four O'Clock Faculty* helps me share my thinking with the world, it's also a deeply personal activity. Blogging helps me document my thoughts. If I visit the Four O'Clock Faculty website, I can look back on a history of what I was thinking at a certain point in time or when I was taking a certain action. It is a therapeutic process and provides me a chance to reflect upon my own growth over time. Blogging also can help educators model to their students what good writing and appropriate sharing look like.

You just learned about some great examples of how professional learning time can be utilized to create something worthwhile. Now, it's your turn. Right now is the perfect time to start something meaningful. Whether you decide to blog or join Twitter or create an awesome learning experience for your students, the time is right.

Summary

- Professional development time doesn't always have to relate to direct learning. Utilizing the time to create something meaningful can also be a valuable use of time.

- Scheduling a Genius Hour during a staff PD opportunity can give everyone the necessary time to pursue their passions.

- FedEx Day provides the opportunity for staff members to collaborate, create, and share. Anything produced during this activity should be useful and shared with colleagues.

- Blogging can provide an outlet for your creative endeavors and can serve as a reflection tool for you.

Reflection Questions

What are you passionate about that you can implement with your students? What can you create alongside students?

_____

_____

_____

_____

If given time at your next staff meeting, what would you create, and how would you share it with colleagues?

_____

_____

_____

_____

What have you been waiting to do? What one thing do you want to start today in order to create something meaningful?

_____

_____

_____

_____

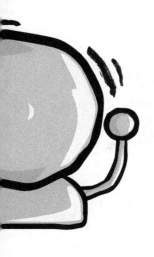

Chapter Ten
Redefining Professional Learning Communities

Alone we are smart.
Together we are brilliant.

—STEVEN W. ANDERSON

A lot of what we have learned so far has been about what you, as an individual educator, can do to improve professional development. But imagine what we could accomplish collectively if we were to commit to work together toward a common goal. I think a good place to start is our professional learning community (PLC).

In some school districts, staff members are required to meet as part of a PLC. While some districts may define PLCs differently from others, the basic idea is that there is dedicated time for staff members to come together to learn. In many instances, the meetings might be monthly or quarterly, and teachers are allowed to choose the topics for discussion. In some cases, teachers are asked to pick a focus for the year or gather to discuss data related to student learning. In many cases, the PLC exists in name only and for compliance purposes.

Teachers are not provided with an agenda, any guidance, and little direction for the professional learning that should take place. If you find yourself in this position, being forced to meet with colleagues, you may want to revamp your PLC.

Try these strategies for repurposing the time utilized during PLCs:

Teacher Choice and Learning Badges

Professional Learning Communities can utilize time to choose topics that are relevant to their everyday roles. Teachers might be able to choose from a list of topics created by the school or district (or add their own), discuss and share (possibly through Twitter and Voxer), and earn a digital badge based on the content they are able to master. This would be demonstrated with a learning or performance task based on work they are doing in the classroom. This type of relevancy allows for teachers to directly impact instruction for their students; for example, if a group of teachers in the building is looking to improve formative assessment techniques, then using PLC time to research and find alternative assessment strategies would be a good use of time. Teachers might connect with experts on Twitter or read several articles or blog posts on the topic and then bring back the results and share. At the end of the day, if teachers can demonstrate that the research has made a positive impact on instruction in the classroom, then teachers would earn an Assessment Expert badge. These badges might be digital, although I've also seen several districts successfully create a culture of learning by posting actual badges outside of teachers' doors, letting everyone know what it is in which they are an expert. (A simple laminated paper copy hanging outside of a classroom works well!) The benefit of this is that colleagues may realize someone is an expert in something about which they are trying to learn—and they connect to learn.

Lesson Study

When professional development is job-embedded, it has a greater likelihood of helping an educator to impact learning. Try using PLC time to conduct a lesson study. This one can be tricky depending on when PLC meetings are held. In my current school, PLC meetings are held during the school day, with each teacher getting a substitute to cover their class for the day. This type of structure works perfectly for a lesson study. Work with colleagues to decide who is going to teach the lesson. Consider trying out a new technique or strategy. Think of this as a learning lab where you are trying something, and failure is a likely possibility. The key here, however, is that several colleagues will observe and provide critical feedback after the lesson. This part is important. Make sure that you always leave time after a lesson observation for colleagues to debrief, talk over the lesson, ask questions, and provide constructive criticism.

"I thought it worked really well when you…"

"I think the students checked out when…"

"Next time, you may want to try…"

As colleagues observe, they may want to use a simple reporting protocol to help provide feedback and constructive criticism. One that might work is having teachers ready to share three things about the observed lesson:

Something that worked well

Something upon which to improve

Something to consider next time

At first it may feel uncomfortable for teachers to be observed by colleagues, but if this type of activity is infused as part of a professional learning culture, the information gleaned from peer observations will be extremely valuable in helping to improve instruction, try out/workshop new strategies or techniques, or simply see what other teachers might be doing. One of the professional learning traps that many educators fall into is isolation. The best educators learn from each other, so get out there and watch and learn from each other!

Data Dump

We have all heard—ad nauseam—about data-based decision making in education and the use of data walks or data walls. I believe there is one key step that is missing in how most schools and districts approach the use of data. Now, I am a self-professed data geek. I enjoy using Excel and Google Sheets. I've accepted geek-ness and am willing to share my passion for data with others.

Most educators are inundated with data, and many are intimidated by it.

Benchmark assessments, online assessments, standardized testing data, formative and summative assessments; the list can go on and on. Most educators don't know what to do with data. And it's not their fault. They've never been properly trained in analyzing data. No one has ever sat with them and asked the question, "What does it all mean?" Where schools are failing with the use of data is looking at information about students and turning it into actionable steps to move learning forward. How do we fix this?

Use your PLC time to conduct a Data DUMP. I know, I know. It just sounds awesome! Again, data analysis may not be all that sexy to some people, but valuable information can be gleaned from worthwhile analysis. So here are a few, simple steps:

1. **Discuss.** Look at the data and talk about it. Are there any trends that might be obvious? Are there any trends that are less obvious? Are particular students doing well—or not so well? Which students need the most help and the most resources?

Start your discussion by asking lots of questions, and continue the discussion by asking more questions. Write all of the questions down on a large piece of poster paper. No question is too specific or minute of a detail. Talk about what you see in the data.

2. **Understand.** After generating many questions, the next step is to ask a Final Question: "What does it all mean?" This is the part where you try to answer some of those questions you generated during Step 1. You also ask a follow-up question: "Why?" Why are students in Group X doing so well? Why are students in Group Z doing so poorly? Try to understand the causes of the data. Try to recognize in some cases that the "trend" you see may be an anomaly. The key is understanding what the data is telling you.

3. **Make Plans.** Step 3 is the most important and often the step that many educators skip or forget to complete. Now that you've looked at the data and identified some key trends, and you understand why those trends might be happening, how will you fix it? Write down actionable steps that will help improve instruction and learning. Here's how the discussion might start:

> "Students in Group Z are performing poorly because they are not reading or being read to over the summer. We are not providing enough support to parents in order to prevent summer-reading slide. So what steps are we going to take to make sure this group does not experience summer-reading slide during the upcoming summer transition?"

By following the three easy steps of a Data DUMP, data can be used efficiently and effectively. Again, we must capitalize on the PLC time that teachers are given and ensure meaningful, relevant discussion is happening during this time.

Summary

- Professional Learning Communities, when done right, can provide the opportunity for educators to grow as learners and to improve instruction for students.

- Digital learning badges can motivate teachers to participate in a learning community based on choice. Teachers choose the topics about which they will learn and how they will learn them.

- Using PLC time to conduct a lesson study can help educators see what quality instruction looks like. The feedback loop can help those being observed as well as those doing the observing.

- Teachers are overwhelmed with data, and are often unable to understand or analyze it due to a lack of training. A simple Data DUMP can help you reflect and make changes so as to improve instruction.

Reflection Questions

Do you meet regularly with a professional learning community? Are the activities worthwhile in helping you grow as a learner?

_____

_____

_____

_____

What lesson(s) would you be willing to share with colleagues during a lesson study? Which of your colleagues would you like to see teach a lesson?

_____

_____

_____

_____

How can you get better at analyzing data in order to improve instruction? Which colleagues can help you in your quest to get better at understanding data?

_____

_____

_____

_____

Chapter Eleven

Dealing with Disappointing PD

You want to change your life? Control the only thing you can control: the meaning you give something.

—TONY ROBBINS

In the Introduction, I recounted a particularly bad professional development experience in which I found myself virtually trapped in a writing workshop that I was sure was doing me no good whatsoever. During that workshop, and even for a few years afterward, I complained long and loud about what a waste of time it was for me, a math teacher, to sit through a class on a new writing assessment. But the truth is, I was wrong. While it certainly was not the best use of my time, I did learn some useful things about writing. I was able to absorb new information and apply it to my profession. In fact, years later when I moved into administration and found myself overseeing a wide range of subjects, I wished I had paid closer attention. It presented me with an interesting dilemma—although that particular workshop wasn't meaningful or relevant to me at the time, it became just that several years later. What if I hadn't paid any attention during that workshop? I have to wonder if the task of creating #4OCF might have been more challenging. So I guess the moral of the story is, we all have a responsibility to make the best of every situation, and when we do, the outcome can be positive.

The truth is, all educators will have professional development experiences that are terrible. Let's set the scene: Ten minutes and three PowerPoint slides into a session, the presenter asks a question, but doesn't wait for a response. He simply begins reading the next slide word for word. You notice a colleague at the end of your cafeteria bench nodding off, ready to get in some well-deserved shut-eye. Another colleague has checked out and is surfing websites on his phone. An administrator sits at the front of the room, checking email on her tablet. As you focus your attention back on the presenter, he brings up a slide promoting active learning and drones on about engaging students using active learning techniques. You decide at this point, twenty minutes into the session, that you cannot sit there any longer. You could get up and leave, but someone would probably notice, and besides, you are contractually required to be there. Here are your options, as I see it:

1. **Tune out.** This option is basically the equivalent of giving up. You sit and stew silently about how miserable you are, thinking about everything else you could and would rather be doing. If you practice mindfulness, you might be able to completely tune out while still appearing interested in the content, but it's hard to do. Through the years, thanks to sitting through hundreds of professional development sessions, I have noticed that tuned-out educators really do make the worst audiences. Once we tune out, we tend to engage in side conversations, sometimes talking loudly to our neighbors. It's almost as if

many of us have been so prone to students engaging in side conversations that we have accepted it as an appropriate part of listening. It's not. Just as we teach our students to be respectful while someone else is speaking, we all should do the same during workshops and classes we feel are a waste of our time.

2. **Sit and listen.** You actually can relax and try to absorb something that will impact your students and their learning. It might be something small like a teaching strategy or a lesson format you have never tried. Maybe the presenter will say something that will spark your curiosity or creativity. Remember: Although the content of the presentation might not be relevant to you at that moment, there is the possibility it could be helpful to you at some point in the future. Learning is learning, no matter when. It's even possible that you might learn something that you should never do. Maybe the takeaway is as simple as, "I should make sure I never try to help students learn by standing and talking at them for an entire hour."

3. **Be productive.** Face it, you're a captive audience. But even captives can get things done. So resolve to use the time productively. Grab your phone or laptop and open Twitter. Find resources and professional learning that will be relevant to your role. At most conferences or professional development sessions that I attend, I usually bring my trusty laptop and share resources via social media as I am listening to the presentation. Even if you don't have the liveliest presenter, you still might hear something worth sharing online. And who knows? Another professional might benefit from the information you pass on.

4. **Ask questions.** If you feel yourself starting to drift, get vocal. Ask questions of the presenter. Some presenters wait until the end of their session to ask for questions. I always try to take questions throughout my sessions because I don't want people to forget them before the end. Another idea is to have some sticky notes within reach, and you can jot down your questions during the presentation.

5. **Issue a challenge.** It's tricky, but you can openly challenge the presenter. This action can be difficult to pull off but, if conducted with respect, it can prove productive. Above all, tread lightly and choose your battle wisely. But if you disagree with what a presenter is saying, speak up. As an empowered professional learner, you have a voice, and it is your right to use that voice. Let's say you are forced to sit in a session on math instruction in which the presenter is sharing drill-and-kill strategies that she promises will improve standardized test scores. As an experienced educator, you know these strategies will take students only so far and that authentic real-world problems are really the way to go. You might be able to shift the conversation by simply asking the question, "If my students have already mastered their facts, how can I incorporate authentic real-world problem solving to get them thinking critically?" Asking the question in this manner conveys respect and allows the presenter to pivot. But be prepared. The presenter might plant her feet and not budge an inch. She might go right back to spouting ideas that you find unhelpful.

6. **Steer yourself.** If you find yourself in an Edcamp-style setting, you can exercise the Rule of Two Feet. If you are unhappy with a presentation, or it is not quite meeting your needs or

expectations, you can rise on your two feet, exercise your vote about the session, and leave. Find another session that is more relevant or meaningful. Find a colleague with whom you can have a substantial conversation. If there are no other sessions going on at that time, jump online and continue your learning. As Dr. Seuss said, "You have brains in your head. You have feet in your shoes. You can steer yourself any direction you choose."

In the case of any professional development that falls short, educators no longer have to "sit and get." You have options. You have a voice. You have a choice. Don't just sit and take it. Make the best of a bad situation, and your students will be better for it.

Summary

- There are always going to be professional development sessions that are disappointing. Remember that you have no control over them (in most cases). You can only control how you react to them.

- You can simply tune out. This will lead to you learning nothing.

- You can sit and listen. Hopefully, you will learn something.

- Be productive. Use the time to get something done, like finding and sharing resources.

- Ask questions. Find out specifics and generate critical thinking through questioning.

- Speak up and challenge the presenter. This one might feel the best in the moment, but can still be tricky to pull off respectfully.

- Steer yourself. Ultimately, if you are not getting what you need, exercise your choice and find something that will impact your learning.

Reflection Questions

Have you ever been in a bad PD session? What did you do?
How did you react?

_____

_____

_____

_____

How do you best learn during a bad PD session? What
activity could you employ to make sure that the time is not
lost?

_____

_____

_____

_____

Knowing what bad PD can look like, how would you plan a
professional learning session to avoid people fleeing?

_____

_____

_____

_____

Chapter Twelve

Creating the Game Plan

Everyone has a plan until they get punched in the mouth.

—Mike Tyson

Along your professional journey, you will encounter count-less roadblocks that can slow your progress. (For those *Braveheart* fans out there, "They may take our lives, but they'll never take our FREEDOM!) These obstacles have the potential to derail our professional learning goals and always should be taken seriously. We have discussed many of them—lack of time, angry administrators, uncommitted colleagues, state and local mandates—and though they are formidable, they can be conquered. My hope is that this book has given you almost everything you need to take a step forward in your own professional learning and find ways to work around the obsta-cles when they appear on your path. You have learned about several ideas to freshen up professional development in your own learning environment and many ways to engage yourself and your colleagues. Now it's time to devise a game plan. I consider it the true purpose of this book. If we are going to revolutionize education through professional development, we must be systematic in our approach. We must have a plan.

I suggest following these six steps to draft your plan:

1. Start small.

- Commandeer a faculty meeting or brief professional development session. If you are an administrator or in a position of power, you should have no problem using one faculty meeting for the sake of improved professional learning. If you are a teacher, however, this task might be slightly more difficult. To take over a faculty meeting, you first must convince the powers that be that your idea is a good one.

- Choose one of the strategies from the book about which you are passionate and present it to your administrator. Start with something relatively easy such as a Problem-Solving Summit or an Appy Hour. Show your administrator how excited you are about the possibilities for staff learning.

2. Follow up.

- After a successful meeting, follow up with staff.

- Provide resources and help with new tech or apps. If you hosted a problem-solving summit, be sure to share the solutions with the staff members who attended. Follow-up will show colleagues that you are committed to changing professional development for the better.

- If you are a teacher, have a follow-up conversation with your administrator. Let your administrator know how much the staff enjoyed (and took away from) the session. Take time to relay staff reactions and include updates on how teachers are using their new skills and knowledge in the classroom.

Angry Administrator Update

Planning meaningful faculty meetings each month can be a lot of work, and many administrators likely would welcome a staff member's request to help out with one or two meetings during the year. One of our recent staff meetings was put together by our media specialist and featured several of our special-area teachers. Physical education, Spanish, and math joined forces to share some amazing technology and apps with the rest of the staff. It was an amazing experience, and it all started when the media specialist approached me to turn our next staff meeting into a "library open house." Don't forget, if your administrator says no, you might need to go ROGUE and find your learning elsewhere.

3. Continue to develop yourself.

- To help your colleagues learn, you must continue to learn. Find different ways to engage yourself, starting with social media. I also recommend checking out #4OCF.

A. Join a Twitter chat.

B. Read a blog or educational website daily.

C. Read a book with great ideas.

D. Share a copy of a blog post or article you've read with colleagues.

4. Host other voluntary sessions.

- Start with a Twitter 101 workshop.

- Microlearning sessions in which educators can engage in short, focused learning opportunities.

- #TechMexTuesday, to introduce the latest websites and apps.

- Lunch and Learn or Five Minute PD, to use available time.

- ROGUE PD, if you feel like you are not getting what you need.

Basically, any other ideas that might stick to the wall.

These sessions will give you the opportunity to expose your staff members to excellent professional development but also will give you a sense of who's ready for the revolution. The people who show up regularly to your voluntary sessions are your people. They are ready and willing to help in changing the game. Keep in mind that one crazy person redefining professional development is just that—a crazy person. Two crazy people redefining professional development? That's a movement!

5. Promote. Promote. Promote.

- Spread the word about your voluntary sessions.

- Take pictures and share them.

- Tweet out information and links.

- Talk about it with everyone you know.

- Email staff information to let them know what they are missing.

- The PD revolution starts from the ground up and requires a lot of footwork. Don't give up if only two or three people show up. Make sure those three people learn something meaningful, and share with those colleagues who didn't or couldn't show up. If you are demonstrating to others that meaningful, relevant work is taking place, people eventually will attend. Just like in *Field of Dreams*, "If you build it, they will come."

6. **Become a decision maker.** As you begin to lead voluntary and relevant professional development sessions, colleagues will begin to see you as something of an expert. Use what you know to help guide the vision for professional learning in your school or district.

- Join the professional development committee.

- Lead the charge to host an Edcamp in your district.

- Some districts have professional development planning groups that are responsible for in-house development. Make sure you have a seat at the table, and share your ideas.

Leading doesn't always have to function from the top down. You can be a teacher, coach, aide, administrator, or parent. Anyone can lead in the professional learning game. Just join the team and use your voice.

Conclusion

You can only trust yourself and the first six Black Sabbath albums.

—HENRY ROLLINS

Now that you are almost finished with this book, here is my plea: I want you to continue on this journey as part of the Four O'Clock Faculty. I want you to be so committed to your students and your own learning that you take responsibility for changing professional development in your setting. I want you to take action. Host a ROGUE meeting in your classroom. Organize a school-wide or district-wide Edcamp. Organize a jam session for some of your closest friends and colleagues. Connect with educators outside of your school or district to find new ways to engage learners. Sit by yourself and read a book or a blog. Wherever you are and whatever you do, whether you are an administrator or teacher or instructional coach, remember that the best thing you can do to improve learning for your students is to improve learning for yourself.

I believe the only way we can improve professional development is to change our concept of professional development. With the integration of technology, we are no longer limited by time and space. By providing choice, we can engage educators in sessions they consider to be meaningful and relevant to what they do on a daily basis. We can start the process of changing instructional practices within our classrooms. While these models for professional development serve as an introductory method for transforming teaching and learning, there are millions of ways they can be improved.

Let's continue to expand our definition of professional learning, giving ourselves more choices and options, incorporating various learning styles, modeling the type of learning that should be happening with our students, and providing continuous learning sessions, so everyone can learn in great depth. For professional development to be effective, it must be designed to engage educators on relevant topics. It must be continuous, causing us to transform our practices in the classroom. It's time we take advantage of every opportunity to continue our professional learning, using non-traditional timeframes to develop craft and practice.

For years we have lamented when professional development was boring or irrelevant or didn't meet our needs. We have sat and daydreamed, checked email, surfed the Internet or reviewed student work. We've listened half-heartedly and wished for the hour to be over. And to what end? How did any of that help? Through the years, I've learned that when it comes to your own professional learning, there is only one person whom you can trust: yourself.

There is only one way to do professional development if you want it done right. Do it yourself. Turn the DIY movement into the PDIY movement. That's right. PDIY (Professionally Develop It Yourself). It's the only way to go. And right now is the time to go. This is the part where you commit to becoming a part of the Four O'Clock Faculty movement and deciding how to PDIY.

You've read about ways to improve professional development. You've seen the game plan. Now it's time for you to decide. Are you going to sit idly by and let professional development be done *to* you? Or will you join the Four O'Clock Faculty and do it yourself? If you've read this entire book, my hope is that you are moving forward with option two. To facilitate your own professional learning, I have provided you with a concrete way to commit. On the next page, there is space to list the first five steps you will take to improve professional learning for yourself. Don't let this be the part of the book that you skip. Don't say, "I'll do it later." We all know later rarely comes. Trust yourself. Trust me. Take the leap. Write down your steps and then make them happen.

Thank you for taking this journey with me. Thank you for joining the mission. Let's change the face of professional learning for educators together. It is time to make this happen.

My Steps to Changing Professional Learning

What five steps will I take immediately to change the look of professional learning?

1. _____

_____

_____

_____

_____

2. _____

_____

_____

_____

_____

3. _____

_____

_____

_____

_____

_____

4. _____

_____

_____

_____

_____

_____

5. _____

_____

_____

_____

_____

_____

Share your list at #4OCF on Twitter!

Find exclusive chapter resources
and more Four O'Clock Faculty
information here:

fouroclockfaculty.com

Bring Rich Czyz
to Your School

Rich Czyz is available for consulting opportunities, speaking engagements, presentations, professional development sessions, speeches, and keynote addresses on a wide range of relevant education topics. He engages audiences, inspiring them to take their learning back to their own educational settings.

Rich specializes in the following topics:

- Personalized Professional Development

- Student Engagement Strategies

- Integrating Technology across the Curriculum

- Educational Leadership

- Positive School Climate and Culture

- Student Ownership, Voice, and Choice

- Using Data to Guide Instruction

Please contact Rich via email to learn more about consulting and speaking opportunities.

richczyz@gmail.com *or*
4oclockfaculty@gmail.com

More From
Dave Burgess Consulting, inc.

Teach Like a PIRATE

Increase Student Engagement, Boost Your Creativity, and Transform Your Life as an Educator

By Dave Burgess (@BurgessDave)

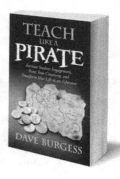

   Teach Like a PIRATE is the New York Times' best-selling book that has sparked a worldwide educational revolution. It is part inspirational manifesto that ignites passion for the profession and part practical road map, filled with dynamic strategies to dramatically increase student engagement. Translated into multiple languages, its message resonates with educators who want to design outrageously creative lessons and transform school into a life-changing experience for students.

Learn Like a PIRATE

Empower Your Students to Collaborate, Lead, and Succeed

By Paul Solarz (@PaulSolarz)

   Today's job market demands that students be prepared to take responsibility for their lives and careers. We do them a disservice if we teach them how to earn passing grades without equipping them to take charge of their education. In *Learn Like a PIRATE*, Paul Solarz explains how to design classroom experiences that encourage students to take risks and explore their passions in a stimulating, motivating, and supportive environment where improvement, rather than grades, is the focus. Discover how student-led classrooms help students thrive and develop into self-directed, confident citizens who are capable of making smart, responsible decisions, all on their own.

P is for PIRATE

Inspirational ABC's for Educators

By Dave and Shelley Burgess (@Burgess_Shelley)

Teaching is an adventure that stretches the imagination and calls for creativity every day! In *P is for PIRATE*, husband and wife team Dave and Shelley Burgess encourage and inspire educators to make their classrooms fun and exciting places to learn. Tapping into years of personal experience and drawing on the insights of more than seventy educators, the authors offer a wealth of ideas for making learning and teaching more fulfilling than ever before.

Play Like a Pirate

Engage Students with Toys, Games, and Comics.
Make Your Classroom Fun Again!

By Quinn Rollins (@jedikermit)

Yes! School can be simultaneously fun and educational. In *Play Like a Pirate*, Quinn Rollins offers practical, engaging strategies and resources that make it easy to integrate fun into your curriculum. Regardless of the grade level you teach, you'll find inspiration and ideas that will help you engage your students in unforgettable ways.

eXPlore Like a Pirate

Gamification and Game-Inspired Course Design
to Engage, Enrich, and Elevate Your Learners

By Michael Matera (@MrMatera)

Are you ready to transform your classroom into an experiential world that flourishes on collaboration and creativity? Then set sail with classroom game designer and educator Michael Matera as he reveals the possibilities and power of game-based learning. In *eXPlore Like a Pirate*, Matera serves as your experienced guide to help you apply the most motivational techniques of gameplay to your classroom. You'll learn gamification strategies that will work with and enhance (rather than replace) your current curriculum and discover how these engaging methods can be applied to any grade level or subject.

The Innovator's Mindset

Empower Learning, Unleash Talent,
and Lead a Culture of Creativity

By George Couros (@gcouros)

The traditional system of education requires students to hold their questions and compliantly stick to the scheduled curriculum. But our job as educators is to provide new and better opportunities for our students. It's time to recognize that compliance doesn't foster innovation, encourage critical thinking, or inspire creativity—and those are the skills our students need to succeed. In *The Innovator's Mindset*, George Couros encourages teachers and administrators to empower their learners to wonder, to explore—and to become forward-thinking leaders.

Master the Media

How Teaching Media Literacy Can
Save Our Plugged-in World

By Julie Smith (@julnilsmith)

Written to help teachers and parents educate the next generation, *Master the Media* explains the history, purpose, and messages behind the media. The point isn't to get kids to unplug; it's to help them make informed choices, understand the difference between truth and lies, and discern perception from reality. Critical thinking leads to smarter decisions—and it's why media literacy can save the world.

The Zen Teacher

Creating FOCUS, SIMPLICITY, and
TRANQUILITY in the Classroom

By Dan Tricarico (@TheZenTeacher)

Teachers have incredible power to influence—even improve—the future. In *The Zen Teacher*, educator, blogger, and speaker Dan Tricarico provides practical, easy-to-use techniques to help teachers be their best—unrushed and fully focused—so they can maximize their performance and improve their quality of life. In this introductory guide, Dan Tricarico explains what it means to develop a Zen practice—something that has nothing to do with religion and everything to do with your ability to thrive in the classroom.

Lead Like a PIRATE

Make School Amazing for Your Students and Staff

By Shelley Burgess and Beth Houf
(@Burgess_Shelley, @BethHouf)

In *Lead Like a PIRATE*, education leaders Shelley Burgess and Beth Houf map out the character traits necessary to captain a school or district. You'll learn where to find the treasure that's already in your classrooms and schools—and how to bring out the very best in your educators. This book will equip and encourage you to be relentless in your quest to make school amazing for your students, staff, parents, and communities.

50 Things You Can Do with Google Classroom

By Alice Keeler and Libbi Miller
(@AliceKeeler, @MillerLibbi)

It can be challenging to add new technology to the classroom, but it's a must if students are going to be well-equipped for the future. Alice Keeler and Libbi Miller shorten the learning curve by providing a thorough over-view of the Google Classroom App. Part of Google Apps for Education (GAfE), Google Classroom was specifically designed to help teachers save time by streamlining the process of going digital. Complete with screenshots, *50 Things You Can Do with Google Classroom* provides ideas and step-by-step instructions to help teachers implement this powerful tool.

50 Things to Go Further with Google Classroom

A Student-Centered Approach

By Alice Keeler and Libbi Miller
(@AliceKeeler, @MillerLibbi)

Today's technology empowers educators to move away from the traditional classroom where teachers lead and students work independently—each doing the same thing. In *50 Things to Go Further with Google Classroom: A Student-Centered Approach*, authors and educators Alice Keeler and Libbi Miller offer inspiration and resources to help you create a digitally rich, engaging, student-centered environment. They show you how to tap into the power of individualized learning that is possible with Google Classroom.

Pure Genius

Building a Culture of Innovation and
Taking 20% Time to the Next Level

By Don Wettrick (@DonWettrick)

For far too long, schools have been bastions of boredom, killers of creativity, and way too comfortable with compliance and conformity. In *Pure Genius*, Don Wettrick explains how collaboration—with experts, students, and other educators—can help you create interesting, and even life-changing, opportunities for learning. Wettrick's book inspires and equips educators with a systematic blueprint for teaching innovation in any school.

140 Twitter Tips for Educators

Get Connected, Grow Your Professional
Learning Network, and Reinvigorate Your Career

By Brad Currie, Billy Krakower, and Scott Rocco
(@bradmcurrie, @wkrakower, @ScottRRocco)

Whatever questions you have about education or about how you can be even better at your job, you'll find ideas, resources, and a vibrant network of professionals ready to help you on Twitter. In *140 Twitter Tips for Educators,* #Satchat hosts and founders of Evolving Educators, Brad Currie, Billy Krakower, and Scott Rocco, offer step-by-step instructions to help you master the basics of Twitter, build an online following, and become a Twitter rock star.

Ditch That Textbook

Free Your Teaching and Revolutionize
Your Classroom

By Matt Miller (@jmattmiller)

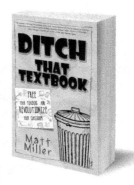

Textbooks are symbols of centuries-old education. They're often outdated as soon as they hit students' desks. Acting "by the textbook" implies compliance and a lack of creativity. It's time to ditch those textbooks—and those textbook assumptions about learning! In *Ditch That Textbook*, teacher and blogger Matt Miller encourages educators to throw out meaningless, pedestrian teaching and learning practices. He empowers them to evolve and improve on old, standard teaching methods. *Ditch That Textbook* is a support system, toolbox, and manifesto to help educators free their teaching and revolutionize their classrooms.

How Much Water Do We Have?

5 Success Principles for Conquering Any
Challenge and Thriving in Times of Change

by Pete Nunweiler with Kris Nunweiler

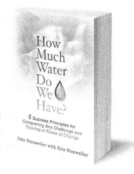

In *How Much Water Do We Have?* Pete Nunweiler identifies five key elements—information, planning, motivation, support, and leadership—that are necessary for the success of any goal, life transition, or challenge. Referring to these elements as the 5 Waters of Success, Pete explains that, like the water we drink, you need them to thrive in today's rapidly paced world. If you're feeling stressed out, overwhelmed, or uncertain at work or at home, pause and look for the signs of dehydration. Learn how to find, acquire, and use the 5 Waters of Success—so you can share them with your team and family members.

Instant Relevance

Using Today's Experiences to Teach Tomorrow's Lessons

By Denis Sheeran (@MathDenisNJ)

Every day, students in schools around the world ask the question, "When am I ever going to use this in real life?" In *Instant Relevance*, author and keynote speaker Denis Sheeran equips you to create engaging lessons *from* experiences and events that matter to your students. Learn how to help your students see meaningful connections between the real world and what they learn in the classroom—because that's when learning sticks.

The Classroom Chef

Sharpen Your Lessons. Season Your Classes.
Make Math Meaningful.

By John Stevens and Matt Vaudrey
(@Jstevens009, @MrVaudrey)

In *The Classroom Chef*, math teachers and instructional coaches John Stevens and Matt Vaudrey share their secret recipes, ingredients, and tips for serving up lessons that engage students and help them "get" math. You can use these ideas and methods as-is, or better yet, tweak them and create your own enticing educational meals. The message the authors share is that, with imagination and preparation, every teacher can be a classroom chef.

Start. Right. Now.

Teach and Lead for Excellence

By Todd Whitaker, Jeff Zoul, and Jimmy Casas
(@ToddWhitaker, @Jeff_Zoul, @casas_jimmy)

In their work leading up to *Start. Right. Now.*, Todd Whitaker, Jeff Zoul, and Jimmy Casas studied educators from across the nation and discovered four key behaviors of excellence: Excellent leaders and teachers *Know the Way, Show the Way, Go the Way, and Grow Each Day*. If you are ready to take the first step toward excellence, this motivating book will put you on the right path.

The Writing on the Classroom Wall

How Posting Your Most Passionate Beliefs about Education Can Empower Your Students, Propel Your Growth, and Lead to a Lifetime of Learning

By Steve Wyborney (@SteveWyborney)

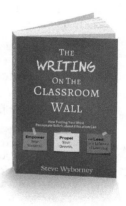

In *The Writing on the Classroom Wall*, Steve Wyborney explains how posting and discussing Big Ideas can lead to deeper learning. You'll learn why sharing your ideas will sharpen and refine them. You'll also be encouraged to know that the Big Ideas you share don't have to be profound to make a profound impact on learning. In fact, Steve explains, it's okay if some of your ideas fall *off* the wall. What matters most is sharing them.

LAUNCH

Using Design Thinking to Boost Creativity and Bring Out the Maker in Every Student

By John Spencer and A.J. Juliani
(@spencerideas, @ajjuliani)

Something happens in students when they define themselves as *makers* and *inventors* and *creators*. They discover powerful skills—problem-solving, critical thinking, and imagination—that will help them shape the world's future ... *our* future. In *LAUNCH*, John Spencer and A.J. Juliani provide a process that can be incorporated into every class at every grade level ... even if you don't consider yourself a "creative teacher." And if you dare to innovate and view creativity as an essential skill, you will empower your students to change the world—starting right now.

Kids Deserve It!

Pushing Boundaries and Challenging
Conventional Thinking

By Todd Nesloney and Adam Welcome
(@TechNinjaTodd, @awelcome)

In *Kids Deserve It!*, Todd and Adam encourage you to think big and make learning fun and meaningful for students. Their high-tech, high-touch, and highly engaging practices will inspire you to take risks, shake up the status quo, and be a champion for your students. While you're at it, you just might rediscover why you became an educator in the first place.

Escaping the School Leader's Dunk Tank

How to Prevail When Others Want to See You Drown

By Rebecca Coda and Rick Jetter
(@RebeccaCoda, @RickJetter)

No school leader is immune to the effects of discrimination, bad politics, revenge, or ego-driven coworkers. These kinds of dunk-tank situations can make an educator's life miserable. By sharing real-life stories and insightful research, the authors (who are dunk-tank survivors themselves) equip school leaders with the practical knowledge and emotional tools necessary to survive and, better yet, avoid getting "dunked."

Teaching Math with Google Apps

50 G Suite Activities

By Alice Keeler and Diana Herrington
(@AliceKeeler, @mathdiana)

Google Apps give teachers the opportunity to interact with students in a more meaningful way than ever before, while G Suite empowers students to be creative, critical thinkers who collaborate as they explore and learn. In *Teaching Math with Google Apps*, educators Alice Keeler and Diana Herrington demonstrate fifty different ways to bring math classes to the twenty-first century with easy-to-use technology.

Your School Rocks...So Tell People!

*Passionately Pitch and Promote the
Positives Happening on Your Campus*

By Ryan McLane and Eric Lowe
(@McLane_Ryan, @EricLowe21)

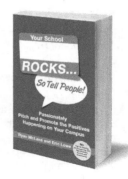

Great things are happening in your school every day. The problem is, no one beyond your school walls knows about them. School principals Ryan McLane and Eric Lowe want to help you get the word out! In *Your School Rocks ... So Tell People!*, McLane and Lowe offer more than seventy immediately actionable tips along with easy-to-follow instructions and links to video tutorials. This practical guide will equip you to create an effective and manageable communication strategy using social media tools. Learn how to keep your students' families and community connected, informed, and excited about what's going on in your school.

Table Talk Math

*A Practical Guide for Bringing Math
into Everyday Conversations*

By John Stevens (@Jstevens009)

Making math part of families' everyday conversations is a powerful way to help children and teens learn to love math. In *Table Talk Math*, John Stevens offers parents (and teachers!) ideas for initiating authentic, math-based conversations that will get kids to notice and be curious about all the numbers, patterns, and equations in the world around them.

Shattering the Perfect Teacher Myth

6 Truths That Will Help You THRIVE as an Educator

By Aaron Hogan (@aaron_hogan)

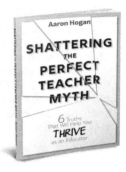

The idyllic myth of the perfect teacher perpetuates unrealistic expectations that erode self-confidence and set teachers up for failure. Author and educator Aaron Hogan is on a mission to shatter the myth of the perfect teacher by equipping educators with strategies that help them shift out of survival mode and THRIVE.

Shift This!

How to Implement Gradual Changes for MASSIVE Impact in Your Classroom

By Joy Kirr (@JoyKirr)

Establishing a student-led culture that isn't focused on grades and homework but on individual responsibility and personalized learning may seem like a daunting task—especially if you think you have to do it all at once. But significant change is possible, sustainable, and even easy when it happens little by little. In *Shift This!* educator and speaker Joy Kirr explains how to make gradual shifts—in your thinking, teaching, and approach to classroom design—that will have a massive impact in your classroom. Make the first shift today!

Unmapped Potential

An Educator's Guide to Lasting Change

By Julie Hasson and Missy Lennard (@PPrincipals)

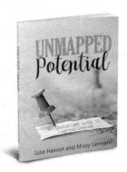

No matter where you are in your educational career, chances are you have, at times, felt overwhelmed and overworked. Maybe you feel that way right now. If so, you aren't alone. But the more important news is that things can get better! You simply need the right map to guide you from frustrated to fulfilled. *Unmapped Potential* offers advice and practical strategies to help you find your unique path to becoming the kind of educator—the kind of person—you want to be.

Social LEADia

Moving Students from Digital Citizenship to Digital Leadership

By Jennifer Casa-Todd (@JCasaTodd)

Equipping students for their future begins by helping them become digital leaders now. In our networked society, students need to learn how to leverage social media to connect to people, passions, and opportunities to grow and make a difference. *Social LEADia* addresses the need to shift the conversations at school and at home from digital citizenship to digital leadership.

Spark Learning

3 Keys to Embracing the Power of Student Curiosity

By Ramsey Musallam (@ramusallam)

Inspired by his popular TED Talk "3 Rules to Spark Learning," this book combines brain science research, proven teaching methods, and Ramsey's personal story to empower you to improve your students' learning experiences by inspiring inquiry and harnessing its benefits. If you want to engage students in more interesting and effective learning, this is the book for you.

Ditch That Homework

Practical Strategies to Help Make Homework Obsolete

By Matt Miller and Alice Keeler
(@jmattmiller, @alicekeeler)

In *Ditch That Homework*, Matt Miller and Alice Keeler discuss the pros and cons of homework, why teachers assign it, and what life could look like without it. As they evaluate the research and share parent and teacher insights, the authors offer a convincing case for ditching homework and replacing it with more effective and personalized learning methods.

About the Author

Rich Czyz started his educational career in 2003 as a fifth-grade teacher. During his time in the classroom, he forced his principal to remove all of the desks from his room (in favor of tables) and angered textbook fans everywhere by simply leaving the books on a shelf and not using them. In roles as a basic skills teacher and instructional coach, Rich continued to push the boundaries, implementing new technology and finding better ways to do things. As an administrator, he first served as a curriculum supervisor and director of curriculum, where he learned that sometimes challenging the status quo is really the only way to do things. Rich currently serves as principal of the Thomas Richards School in New Jersey, where he enjoys participating in kickball games with students.

Rich is the co-founder of the *Four O'Clock Faculty* blog for educators looking to improve instruction and learning for themselves and their students. Rich is passionate about engaging all stakeholders in meaningful and relevant learning. He is an author, blogger, and presenter. Learn more about Rich by following him on Twitter or visiting the blog.

@RACzyz

fouroclockfaculty.com

CPSIA information can be obtained
at www.ICGtesting.com
Printed in the USA
FFHW01n0956180918
48376763-52251FF